EDUCATIONAL ASSESSMENT OF IMMIGRANT PUPILS

EDUCATIONAL ASSESSMENT OF IMMIGRANT PUPILS

Judith M. Haynes, PhD

Formerly research officer, NFER

National Foundation
for Educational
Research in
England and Wales

*Published by the National Foundation for Educational Research
in England and Wales*

*Registered Office: The Mere, Upton Park, Slough, Bucks, SL1 2DQ
London Office: 79 Wimpole Street, London, W1M 8EA*

*Book Publishing Division: 2 Jennings Buildings, Thames Avenue,
Windsor, Berks, SL4 1QS*

First Published 1971

© *National Foundation for Educational Research
in England and Wales, 1971*

SBN   901225   71   1

Cover design by
PETER GAULD, FSIA

Printed in Great Britain by
KING, THORNE & STACE LTD., SCHOOL ROAD, HOVE, SUSSEX

Acknowledgements

I FIRST wish to acknowledge my great debt to the Leverhulme Trust. But for their generous financial support this project might not have become established under the auspices of the National Foundation for Educational Research and I have been sincerely grateful for their continued assistance throughout this investigation.

I am also extremely grateful to my colleagues at the National Foundation for Educational Research for their very ready help and encouragement during the course of this work. In particular I wish to express my gratitude to Dr. S. Wiseman and Dr. D. Pidgeon for their very considerable guidance concerning every aspect of the research and to Miss J. Tarryer for her advice and assistance in carrying out the statistical analysis and for contributing a statistical appendix to this report.

My thanks are also due to Mrs. J. Barker Lunn for her very valuable help in the construction of the teachers' attitude scale and Mrs. E. Thorne who helped me so much in administering and scoring many of the intelligence tests.

Professor P. E. Vernon and subsequently Dr. W. H. King, my tutors at London University Institute of Education, have given much guidance in the design and presentation of the research for a higher degree and I am sincerely grateful for the experience I gained from working under their supervision.

I am indebted also to many Chief Education Officers for granting me permission to interview teachers in their schools and particularly to Mr. Ayres, Chief Education Officer for the London Borough of Ealing, for granting me permission to select the children for the research from the schools in that Borough.

I would also like to thank the teachers themselves for extending so much of their time and interest during my visits to their schools and for their assistance in collecting so much essential data.

Throughout this research a great many friends and colleagues have contributed suggestions and much practical help. Their kind co-operation and support has not only made this investigation possible, but has served to make it a most rewarding experience for the author.

December, 1970   J. M. H.

Contents

Current research and culturally disadvantaged children; previous research into the cross-cultural assessment of ability; the prediction of the educational progress of non-immigrant and immigrant children; non-verbal tests; the translation of verbal tests; practice tests; measuring the ability to learn; the need to assess an immigrant child's ability; the present investigation.

Aims; design of the research; selection of samples; pupil variables; school, class and teacher variables.

Discovering suitable content and presentation of the tests; rationale behind the type of task selected for the learning tests; brief description of the tests; reliability of the learning tests; selection of the scoring methods of the learning ability tests; selected scoring methods.

Concurrent and predictive validity (Indian children); predictive validity (English children); comparative data on initial test scores and subsequent attainment; correlations between the teachers' estimates of ability and subsequent attainment.

Discussion of the results.

Contents

List of Tables

List of Tables

CHAPTER ONE

Introduction

IN recent years an increasing body of literature has appeared on the subject of the immigrant population in Britain. In consequence a greater understanding of the cultural backgrounds and everyday life of the various immigrant groups is available to us, together with some account of their particular needs and of the corresponding gaps in our social services. With facts as our guide it is now possible to make a more sound assessment of the priorities for research, and the present study is an attempt to go some way towards fulfilling one of the research priorities in the educational field.

This first chapter provides an account of the research and literature already available on the subject of assessing the abilities of people from different cultures. It also aims to convey the rationale behind the approach adopted by the present investigation.

1. Current research and culturally disadvantaged children

The rise in numbers of immigrant children attending schools in this country during the last decade is well known. Statistics first became available in 1967, the year in which the Department of Education and Science published the returns of Form 7.i. This form, which is a supplement to the customary annual return of all pupils was first circulated to schools in England and Wales in 1966. The supplement is in two parts. The first section asks for information about numbers of immigrant children and their country of origin and the reports show how the children are distributed among the Local Education Authorities. The second section asks for information concerning numbers of immigrant children in relation to four grades of language competence and so the information should be useful from the point of view of educational planning. This form is now circulated annually and the full figures are to be found in reports of the Department of Education and Science (DES 1967, 1968, 1969, 1970). The total figures for the years which are currently available are to be found in Table 1.

TABLE 1: *Numbers of immigrant pupils attending maintained schools and in need of special tuition in England and Wales*

YEAR	TOTAL NUMBER OF IMMIGRANT PUPILS	NUMBER OF IMMIGRANT PUPILS IN NEED OF SPECIAL TEACHING
1966	131,043†	32,234
1967	183,776†	41,816
1968	220,212	45,803
1969	249,664	43,927

† Excludes those in schools with 10 immigrant pupils or less

In examining these and any other figures to do with immigrants account must always be taken of the definition of 'immigrant' being used. In this case the children had to satisfy one of two criteria to be classified as immigrant: 1. children born outside the British Isles who have come to this country with or to join parents or guardians whose countries of origin were abroad; 2. children born in the United Kingdom to parents whose countries of origin were abroad and who came to the United Kingdom within the previous ten years.

Another set of figures concerning immigrant pupils became available in 1967 from a different source. Independently of the Department of Education and Science, the Schools Council had sponsored a research project regarding the teaching of English to non-English speaking children and this also resulted in a questionnaire being sent to all local education authorities. Being more concerned with the size of the language problem, the Schools Council questionnaire asked whether English was the child's first or second language regardless of place of birth. The figure of 44,000 children with inadequate English given in the Schools Council Working Paper No. 13, (1967), roughly confirms the figures of immigrant pupils with language difficulties published in the same year by the Department of Education and Science. A more detailed account of both these questionnaires may be found in a survey of the administrative policies for immigrant pupils by Power (1967).

With this increase in numbers of children with language difficulty there is a new emphasis in education on the need for research with children who are disadvantaged, whether by virtue of race or social class, and a more urgent demand is being expressed for information

12

about this very heterogeneous category. Reports of actual research studies, however, are very few indeed. In this country the research concerning immigrant children has been largely concerned with the investigation of their linguistic problems and in this connection the Schools Council Research Project carried out at Leeds University under the direction of June Derrick (1966) has made a major contribution. The main objective of this research was the preparation of teaching materials to help teachers enable pupils whose first language is not English to achieve an adequate command of English. As a result of this work we now have some new teaching materials for non-English speaking pupils and a deeper understanding of the principles and methods involved in teaching English as a foreign language.

A parallel project is the intensive inquiry into the particular language difficulties of West Indian children which was set up at Birmingham University under the leadership of Mr. J. Wight under the auspices of the Schools Council. Also at Birmingham University during 1969-70 was the first year of a project concerned with the development of tests of English for use with immigrant children. This project, financed by CRDML through the Department of Education and Science, spent the first year in reviewing relevant research and tests and preparing specifications for a test battery. The construction, trials and validation of the tests will be carried out at the National Foundation for Educational Research and are expected to continue until 1972.

This work is of great practical value therefore but it is only a part of what is required and there are many other essential questions which need to be explored. For instance we need to know a lot more about the adjustment problems of the different immigrant groups: how to activate the motivation of the children in school; how to facilitate a relationship between home and school from which mutual support and enrichment can be derived; and information is still sadly lacking on the merits of the various administrative and remedial measures which were developed in response to the sudden influx of children from abroad but which may well need revision particularly as local conditions begin to change. With intuition rather than facts as our guide such issues remain controversial and, as the survey of the literature of Goldman and Taylor (1966) indicated, research is still very much in its infancy.

Working as an educational psychologist in an area of London where there were substantial numbers of immigrant children, the writer recognized that another kind of investigation was also urgently needed. This concerns the diagnosis of the basic learning skills and learning difficulties of our immigrant children. The investigations which have so far been carried out in this country in connection with the abilities of immigrant children are few and may be readily summarized.

Alleyne (1962) in his study of the effects of bilingualism on educational attainment in which he compared Welsh, West Indian and English children found appreciable differences in attainment and verbal ability. He also found that the bi-lingual children born outside Britain were undeniably handicapped on a non-verbal group test of intelligence.

Saint (1963) in his assessment of a group of Punjabi boys of secondary school age also found that their mean scores on non-verbal tests of ability were significantly lower than the normative sample, but that there was a positive correlation between their test scores and length of schooling in this country. This study has borne out the relationship between length of schooling in a Western environment and test performance which was first demonstrated by Klineberg's (1935) work in the New York schools with the Negroes who had migrated to the Northern States.

A recent report from the Inner London Education Authority (1967) demonstrates this relationship with much larger numbers of immigrant children. This report is of a survey covering 1,068 immigrant children in 52 primary schools and shows that whereas children who started their English schooling late in their junior stage often had too little time to make much progress and their poor attainments were a serious problem when they transferred to secondary school, the immigrants who had had several years of primary education tended to achieve higher ratings for verbal reasoning, English and mathematics at eleven-plus. It was concluded that there is a definite, though moderate relationship between length of English education and improvement in test performance.

Houghton (1966) studied the relative performance on intelligence tests of West Indian and English children at the infant school level. He found very little difference in their mean scores but the scores of both groups were depressed and it seems likely that the explanation of the scores of the English children should also be sought in terms of their environment deprivation.

Payne (1967) found significant differences between West Indian and English children of seven and eight years of age on standardized tests and has again confirmed the serious handicaps of immigrant children on both verbal and non-verbal tests.

14

In drawing attention to the limiting effects of cultural differences on both verbal and non-verbal test and school performance, these studies all point to the importance of interpreting the test results of immigrant children with extreme caution.

2. Previous research into the cross-cultural assessment of ability

A review of the previous research reveals that in the early years studies were confined to the assessment of non-Europeans on Western-type tests with the inevitable and misleading comparisons of European and non-European IQs. These comparative studies invariably revealed an inferiority on the part of non-Europeans which grows less the more closely the group approximates its way of life to European culture, and the cross-cultural measurement of intelligence became bound up with discussion about the relative importance of heredity and environment as determinants of ability. In the 1950s a new era in the psychological testing of peoples from different cultures began to emerge. Primitive societies were by this time recognized as developing nations and with this came the realization that abilities had to be identified, educated and trained. So in recent years the purpose of psychological testing changed from one of obtaining comparative data to one of introducing selective procedures at various stages of education and training.

a. *The Heredity-Environment Controversy*

The evidence was thoroughly reviewed by Anastasi and Foley (1949, chs. 20, 21 and 22). They concluded that differences in cultural and educational experience accounted for the greater part of the differences observed but this issue is still the subject of impassioned debate and inquiry.

Following the recent provocative article 'How much can we boost IQ and scholastic achievement?' by Jensen (1969) in which some highly controversial conclusions are drawn about the relationship of race and intelligence, casting serious doubts on the possible effectiveness of compensatory education, the Editor of the *Journal of Social Issues* published a statement on Race and Intelligence (1969) which received the unanimous endorsement of the Council of the Society for the Psychological Study of Social Issues. The Council considers that 'statements specifying the hereditary components of intelligence are unwarranted by the present state of scientific knowledge', and they summarize the evidence from four decades of research in these words —'There are marked differences in intelligence test scores when one

15

compares a random sample of whites and Negroes. What is equally clear is that little definite evidence exists that leads to the conclusion that such differences are innate. The evidence points overwhelmingly to the fact that when one compares Negroes and whites of comparable cultural and educational background, differences in intelligence test scores diminish markedly; the more comparable the background, the less the difference. There is no direct evidence that supports the view that there is an innate difference between members of different racial groups. We believe that a more accurate understanding of the contribution of heredity to intelligence will be possible only when social conditions for all races are equal and when this situation has existed for several generations . . . Recent research indicates that environmental factors play a role from the moment of a child's conception. The unborn child develops as a result of a complex, little understood interaction between heredity and environmental factors; this interaction continues throughout life. To construct questions about complex behaviour in terms of heredity versus environment is to over-simplify the essence and nature of human development and behaviour.'

Leaving the premature question of genetic factors in any racial variations in intelligence on one side, we are left in no doubt of the evidence that a depriving environment can stunt intellectual development and that differing backgrounds can encourage the differential development of abilities.

b. *Patterns of Ability*

The most useful questions concerning the role of cultural factors in human ability are questions about 'which conditions give rise to which kinds of learning', and the problem becomes one of describing the patterns of ability which are characteristic of individuals reared in different cultural environments.

The fact that so many investigations have shown that the intelligence test performances of different racial groups are not the same endorses the need for research into the perceptual, manipulative and problem-solving habits of various racial groups. Data concerning different patterns of ability and their cultural background are now becoming available.

Unlike most of the early investigations of cultural differences in ability, Lesser, Fifer and Clark (1965) for example, were interested more in the differential pattern of mental abilities between cultures and they compared the performance of four ethnic groups of six- and seven-year-old children in New York schools: Chinese, Jewish,

16

Negro and Puerto Rican. Using tests of verbal and reasoning ability, number and spatial conceptualization, they found distinct differences in the patterns of ability between the four groups and these patterns of ability did not vary within each group according to social class. Vernon in particular has been concerned with the very considerable task of discovering the various environmental conditions which contribute to different patterns of ability. In his recent book '*Intelligence and Cultural Environment*' (1969) he reports several such investigations with no less than six different cultural groups and he is able to define their characteristic strengths and weaknesses in mental functioning and link these to distinct differences in upbringing and experience. The aim behind Vernon's work is to unearth the means by which the developing countries can be in some way assisted to achieve 'Western Intelligence'. Since the aspirations of the majority of immigrants are in the direction of success and achievement within our society, we too have the similar task of discovering how to make the maximum use of their educational potentialities in the direction of our criteria of success.

It is for this reason that whilst intelligence tests developed within the Western culture favour people brought up within that culture, a strong case can be made for continuing to use these tests with different peoples. Their scores according to the norms already available will give an assessment of their present achievements and *short-term* predictions of their ability to succeed according to our standards.

It is essential to keep in mind, however, that there are severe limitations as to the long-term conclusions that can be drawn from an immigrant child's performance on the tests currently used to predict the educational achievements of non-immigrant children, since they cannot predict his response to the new educational process. The test scores merely tell us how the immigrant child compares with an English child of the same age at this point in time, but they can tell us nothing about his response to a new learning situation.

c. *Factors Affecting the Test Performance of Different Cultural Groups*

Studies of the abilities of different racial and ethnic groups must allow for the selective encouragement of different skills, abilities and patterns of response in the interpretation of test scores. The failure to make allowances for differing work habits, interests and levels of motivation may also give rise to misleading conclusions.

We have been reminded over many years of the important effects of traditional attitudes and behaviour in a test situation by a few investigators who have recorded some quite striking examples. For instance, Porteus (1931), in his testing of Australian aborigines, found it difficult to convince his subjects that they were to solve the questions individually and without assistance. Biesheuvel (1949) demonstrates that it is also virtually impossible to equate motivation for comparative studies in different cultural groups. The competitive spirit is not as strong and speed plays less part in non-European groups. Biesheuvel also found that the method of presenting the tests had a crucial bearing on the results obtained and he found it necessary to devise special methods of demonstration and explanation using a common language.

Scott (1950) in his highly instructive and entertaining account of the first experiments in intelligence testing to be undertaken in the Sudan had also discovered the need to experiment with the method of test presentation so as to find the conditions which would be least affected by irrelevant emotional factors or problems in communication. He found it necessary to familiarize the children with the kind of task which would be expected of them and introduced a 'warming-up period' before the test itself. This also served to reduce the children's fear of a strange white test administrator and helped to put them maximally at ease.

Then there is among other evidence the report of the Northern Mental Ability Survey in Northern Rhodesia (McArthur *et al.* 1964) which indicates that Western-type tests of ability can be valuable for predictive purposes with people in a different culture, provided there has been careful coaching and explanation and adaptation of the tests.

In considering the test performance of immigrant children we must also keep in mind the fundamental effects of factors such as poverty, isolation, malnutrition and lack of intellectual stimulation. Malnutrition is a continuing and increasing problem in under-developed countries. It is known that brain cells are damaged irreversibly by deficiencies in diet before birth and in early infancy and these effects cannot be made up by improved feeding later on. Dietary deficiencies also reduce the child's resistance to disease which in turn reduces the use he is able to make of his abilities.

Moreover we know that learning is cumulative and that later conceptual development rests on prior stages of development in which perception plays a crucial role. There are many studies which report evidence of ethnic group differences in perceptions. One of the earliest cross-cultural psychological studies was carried out by Rivers (1901) in the Torres Strait using the Muller-Lyer and the Horizontal-Vertical illusions. It was found that the natives were less prone to the former and more susceptible to the latter. Similar investigations with the Muller-Lyer illusions have subsequently been made in many parts of the world and there have been several studies which have related the susceptibility to illusions to the physical attributes of the environment and which have shown the relationship between particular styles of living and certain characteristic perceptual processes.

One perceptual characteristic reported from many parts of Africa is a particular difficulty in understanding pictures. Even African pupils who are doing well in secondary schools are often puzzled by pictures in geography and science textbooks, so that we really cannot expect Africans to interpret two dimensional representations in psychological tests according to Western conventions. Wilson (1961), in using film to teach natives in Africa to read, again shows how even in the field of ordinary vision much training is required. They focussed their attention on a part rather than the whole of each picture and failed to follow the story element involved.

Difficulties of visual interpretation have been widely observed, but it is highly doubtful that they have a racial or genetic determinant. McFie (1961) found that on retesting African boys in a technical school after a two-year period they made large increases in speeded tests involving spatial and manipulative abilities. McFie attributes the improved performance on these tests, whilst their verbal test scores remained unchanged, to the effects of their intervening education, which had placed emphasis on drawing and construction, and he considers this to be evidence for the remediability of defects in perception and spatial ability.

We now have a considerable amount of evidence concerning the complexity of factors which can affect test performances and it is now clear that a wide range of factors must be taken into account when considering the test performance of any child whose development has been impoverished by virtue of physical or intellectual limitations in his surroundings. The child already carries a handicap but there are also elements within the testing situation and test itself which may serve to put any child who has been brought up amongst different traditions and educational practices at an even further disadvantage. These considerations have been recently summarized by several authors, notably, Ferron (1965), Butcher (1968), Vernon (1969) and Biesheuvel (1969).

3. The prediction of the educational progress of non-immigrant and immigrant children

Summing up the predictive powers of objective tests Vernon (1957 p. 74) wrote 'As a team the three tests most usually employed yield high correlations with later performance in the grammar school'. The three objective tests to which Vernon refers are tests of verbal intelligence, arithmetic and English. Together these tests normally give correlations in the region of 0·85 with a criterion of success in the secondary school. He goes on to say, however, that in nearly every research there is evidence of the superiority of the intelligence tests as a predictor of later educational success.

Intelligence tests can give accurate predictions of a child's ability to learn even though the tests themselves strive to avoid too heavy a loading in learned materials. They correlate highly with future learning because mental development involves a cumulative process; the best prediction of what anyone will learn in the future is likely to be related to how much he has been able to learn in the past and intelligence tests do measure the child's present stage of development and the extent to which he is able to apply knowledge and skills which he has already learned. Intelligence tests are now generally regarded as tests of general cognitive attainment, but when we go on to say that they are also predictive of future attainment we are assuming that all the people tested, and thereby compared with regard to their potential, have all had an equal opportunity to learn the skills which the test required and become equally familiar with the material which the test items employ. In the case of immigrant children in particular this would clearly be an unwarranted and misleading assumption. Certainly several follow-up studies abroad have cast doubt on the predictive validity of tests of ability originally constructed for use in a different culture.

If we use our existing tests translated or un-translated, verbal or non-verbal, with immigrant children we do not know how to interpret the test scores. We simply do not know what it means in terms of future progress if an immigrant child scores, say, 100 on a particular test. Surely in consideration of his linguistic and other cultural differences this score would be worth more in terms of potential than the same score of an English child on the same test? But how much more? If a culturally disadvantaged child is reported to have a particular score and the score is merely used to describe his present standing with the respect to a specified norm group, no iniquity is involved. It is only when this score in interpreted as meaning that the child ranks or will rank no higher in learning ability than does a native-born child with the same score that our conclusions will almost certainly be erroneous. These considerations are reflected in an increasing tendency for scores on intelligence tests to be linked to an evaluation of the child's previous experience and they are felt to convey little meaning if they are considered out of this context. Assessing the abilities of immigrant children whose background experience is all the harder for us to fully comprehend is even less straightforward.

It might well be said, therefore, that the safest basis we have for assessing the immigrant child's future ability is to observe his present learning ability and the actual progress he makes in acquiring English and his school achievement over as long a period as possible. This is very often all we can do but the drawback is that this is an unstandardized procedure which is affected by the amount and quality of help the child is currently receiving at home and at school as well as by the subjective impressions of teacher and psychologist.

4. Non-verbal tests

In view of the language problem of many of our immigrant children it is frequently thought that the use of non-verbal tests would provide a ready and valid answer.

Certainly the first major attempt to assess the abilities of people from different backgrounds used such tests. This first inquiry was prompted by the first world war when non-verbal group tests were devised for testing foreign-speaking and illiterate soldiers. Similar tests were given during the second world war in the selection of recruits in Africa and India; and in the post-war years non-verbal tests have been devised in some of the under-developed countries to pick out the good trainees for various industries and more skilled types of employment. These tests have been designed to tap the specific skills demanded of employment or training in question and are proving useful in predicting a short-term and local criterion.

Such testing, however, cannot make an assessment of the full educational potentiality of the individual. Butcher (1968, p. 256) in reporting some work of Ortar in Israel, for example, using the Wechsler Intelligence Scale with five groups of children varying in social class and degree of acculturation found that 'Whereas the verbal tests placed all five groups in the expected order, the performance tests, so far from being 'culturally fair', produced greater differences in favour of the more privileged and longer-acculturated children'. Other evidence has been collected which also demonstrates the fallacy of supposing that non-verbal tests are more free from environmental influences than verbal ones.

Verbal and number tests are in general far better predictors of educational achievement than non-verbal or performance tests. But where there is a distinct language deficit, the correlations for verbal tests and subsequent achievement are likely to be reduced and on account of difficulties in communicating the test items non-verbal tests, normally a second best, would appear to be more appropriate for immigrant children with little or no understanding of English.

It must be recognized that not only is performance on non-verbal tests affected by cultural background but that somewhat different abilities or aspects of intelligence are being assessed by two types of test. It was the hope underlying the construction of the so-called culture-free and culture-fair tests of ability that non-verbal test items could serve an equivalent function. We know from many sources that the nearer these pioneers got to their goal of constructing a culture-fair or culture-free test the further away they were from constructing a test which could be used in making educational predictions. The tests did not, in fact, involve good examples of skills relevant to educational progress and the whole approach was clearly based on the concept of intelligence as some fixed power of the mind which would reveal itself through unrelated tasks and in widely differing test situations.

Non-verbal tests have therefore been developed primarily for use with children or adults who cannot properly be assessed with verbal scales. They are used for example with deaf and speech defective children and adults, and appropriate norms have been developed for handicapped groups. But when it comes to interpreting the scores of non-English speaking immigrant children on such tests we are not only using a type of test which does not have a close bearing to the kind of skill involved in school learning but we are still up against the fact that children from different cultures are often at just as much of a disadvantage, and to an unknown degree, on non-verbal as verbal tests.

5. The translation of verbal tests

Two other distinct approaches have been made in the study of the educational potentialities of non-Europeans. One of these is the translation of certain well-known intelligence scales into the language of the people being tested. In the United States, the instructions for group tests of non-verbal ability were translated into Spanish for the purposes of testing the Puerto Rican pupils in New York City, and there have been several translations and revisions of the Binet Scales for use with different European, Asiatic and African Groups.

Bearing in mind the discouraging validity of the culture-free and performance tests in making educational predictions together with Vernon's reminder that the Western yardstick is ultimately the most relevant for evaluating the abilities of all races, it might be argued that this approach of translating and adapting our existing tests should be the one used for testing our immigrant pupils. It might seem that, in order to draw really valid conclusions about their abilities, a restandardization of the tests we use to assess the non-immigrant children in our schools together with an adaptation of translation is indicated and necessary for each cultural group.

Such an undertaking would involve tremendous resources in time and money and the problem of finding appropriately trained people to construct and later administer the tests in the different languages. But even if this could be achieved, the assessments would still be of questionable validity since some immigrant children would still be at more of a disadvantage than others owing to the varying degrees by which they had become estranged from their own cultures and native tongues.

6. Practice tests

The other approach which seems to have been one of the most creative steps towards the construction of tests for immigrant children was taken by Ortar (1960), who began to work on the problem of assessing the learning ability of the new immigrants to Israel in the early 1950s.

Ortar was also working in a situation where it seemed likely that a reliable assessment of a person's ability to absorb new knowledge and skills would be more useful than an evaluation of previous acquired abilities and attainments. Her work has emphasized the point that there is little value to be gained out of assigning a single IQ to a child whose abilities are likely to be undergoing considerable change. Using the kinds of items to be found on conventional intelligence tests, she tried to lessen the effects of inequality of previous experience with the scheme of introducing a period of practice and coaching between an initial testing and a re-test. The final scores tended to be higher than the initial scores and to be correlated more highly with future attainment. Incidentally, it was with this aim of levelling out previous experience that some local education authorities instituted practice tests during their eleven-plus selection procedures. However, the tests which Ortar adapted and constructed for the most part involved practice on the types of item found in non-verbal intelligence tests so that the tests, although being a considerable improvement in a straightforward administration of a non-verbal test, are still somewhat unrelated to the prediction of educational progress.

7. Measuring the ability to learn

Finally, some recent work in the United States carried out by Jensen (1961) should be mentioned. He has developed tests which measure a child's ability to learn and has compared the performance of children from different classes and ethnic groups. He has found that lower class or disadvantaged children, whether they are white, Negro or Mexican, very often do as well on these tests which directly involve learning as do the middle class children.

Jensen (1963) has also shown that children who were classified as retarded on the Stanford-Binet Intelligence Scale (and this again is a most interesting and important finding), may be a very heterogeneous group with regard to actual learning ability. In this study all the seventh, eighth and ninth grade children in one school were classified into three groups according to their IQs on the Stanford-Binet Intelligence Scale. He found a significant association between IQ and learning ability for all three groups but some children, classified as retarded according to their IQ, learned as fast as the gifted children, indicating the usefulness of this kind of test as a potential diagnostic device. Learning ability, as measured by Jensen's technique, is clearly a measure of some important aspect of mental ability not necessarily tapped by the IQ test.

In a subsequent form of his learning test, Jensen and Rohwer (1963) found that when taught to verbalize in the learning situation the learning ability of children classified as retarded in the terms of IQ and school achievement was enhanced. Though learning can take place without verbal mediation, as of course it does in animal learning, it may be exceedingly slow. Until specially instructed, some of the retarded children seemed to learn on this basis, but given help in verbalizing, their performance was immediately facilitated. The crucial role played by verbal mediation processes in mobilizing a child's basic learning ability has been described in detail in Jensen's (1967a) article which is particularly concerned with the experiential deficiencies of the culturally disadvantaged.

In this article Jensen lists these early deficiencies and their effects now witnessed at school. For example he attributes the seemingly inattentive and disruptive hyperactivity of some culturally disadvantaged children to features of the parent-child relationship which are very often characteristic of middle-class children but which have been lacking for these children, such as mutual play accompanied by relevant speech and reading to the child. Jensen emphasized the role of language as of crucial importance as a 'tool of thought' and considers early language deficiencies to be crippling to the child's later intellectual development. Such children are much less likely to talk to themselves as an aid to learning and thinking and he suggests that this is one of the reasons why non-verbal tests are by no means culture-free or culture-fair since they do require private verbal processes such as labelling, the ability to associate, abstract and categorize.

This work endorses the importance of enabling our immigrant children to overcome their language restrictions. It also underlines the validity of measuring the ability to learn amongst disadvantaged groups.

8.   The need to assess an immigrant child's ability

It is clear that there is a great demand and need for suitable tests. Teachers and psychologists naturally want to be able to assess the potential of some of the immigrant children, especially those who seem to be having some difficulty in learning, so that they can have some idea of what kind of response to expect, how much progress and how soon they can be expected to make it. They may be wondering if any of them would be more appropriately placed in a special school or class. These children arrive at our schools speaking a variety of languages and often very little standard English and for the sake of their future we need to be able to make a more sound appraisal of their present educational disabilities. Are their difficulties at school merely temporary so that they can be expected to make good progress once they have become more familiar with their surroundings and in particular have acquired more English, or are their handicaps of a more permanent nature arising perhaps either from a deprived or different upbringing or possibly from innate limitations?

The concept of potential ability is receiving a great deal of attention in current educational discussions. Much knowledge has been accumulated about the factors in the environment which are conducive to more successful performance in school and it is evident that not only immigrant but also pupils native to this country have ability which is not being fully realized. Research is now beginning to go beyond the crude socio-economic variables which influence educational progress to the area of the more subtle psychological aspects of the child's early inter-personal relationships. The most detailed research of this kind was carried out by Bernstein (1961) concerning the relationship of language patterns and cognitive abilities and has been extended by the research of Deutsch (1962) in New York and Hess and Shipman (1965) in Chicago into the area of language behaviour and parent-child interaction. Research in this country, including evidence submitted for the Plowden Report, has demonstrated that parental interest and encouragement are more important in sustaining the child's motivation to learn than the material circumstances of the home.

Once he goes to school the teacher also plays an essential part in maintaining the child's active participation in the learning process. Bloom, Davis and Hess in their book *Compensatory Education for Cultural Deprivation* survey the large amount of experimental literature bearing on factors such as inadequate motivation, health, linguistic handicap, lack of intellectual stimulation in the home or concern for achievement; but they also emphasize the effects of school experiences on the disadvantaged child's self-concept. There is evidence that teachers tend to expect lower-class children to fare worse, having a further depressing effect on their self-esteem. As a result, the deficit in achievement gets progressively worse, giving rise to further deterioration in attitude to school so that with disadvantaged children in particular a really full appraisal of their abilities could make for more positive expectancies and achievement all round.

The relationship between the teacher's attitude and the child's actual progress has recently been much publicized in the report of an experiment carried out by Rosenthal and Jacobson (1968) in the United States. All the children in a large elementary school were given an intelligence test and the teachers were then informed that a few children from each class, who had in fact been selected at random, were about to bloom intellectually and that the teachers could expect them to make marked progress. After a year, further testing revealed that in many classes the selected children had indeed made significant gains. The statistical validity of the results reported in this study have since been criticised (Thorndike, 1968) and are open to question; nevertheless, the study has been of service in drawing attention to the much neglected area of teacher attitude in research.

A survey concerned with teaching French in primary schools carried out by the National Foundation for Educational Research also confirms the effects of teachers' expectancies. A close look was taken at the progress of children of low general ability in relation to their teacher's attitudes. Teachers who felt that French should be taught to dull as well as bright children tended to get much better results with the dull children in their classes and in fact many of the less able children were able to exceed the performance of their more intelligent classmates. This is one of the few studies which provides direct evidence of an association between teacher expectancies and pupil achievement and again we find that relatively low performance on an intelligence test need not necessarily mean an equally poor ability to learn.

In his recent book *Expectation and Pupil Performance*, Pidgeon (1970) discusses this subject in detail. Drawing on the data obtained in the course of a large scale comparative study of the attainments of 13- to 14-year-old children in 12 countries, Pidgeon points out that the range of attainment is greater in England than in any of the other countries involved, a difference which is paralleled within this country by the greater range of attainment in streamed as opposed to unstreamed schools (Barker Lunn 1970). England is one of the few remaining countries with a selective system of education and Pidgeon considers this to be a reflection of a belief, widely held in this country, that intelligence is a fixed and innately determined entity. He interprets the wider range of attainment of English children as being 'to a large extent due to the operation of the self-fulfilling prophecy based on teacher expectations' and endorses Barker Lunn's (1970) conclusion that it is this underlying attitude rather than the actual organization of a school which is important for the educational achievements of its pupils.

The tendency to continue to think in terms of a fixed IQ becomes extremely serious when one is considering the capabilities of immigrant or any disadvantaged children. The teacher's attitude assumes an even greater importance because this is a situation where the teacher may well have a much firmer preconceived idea concerning a child's ability and the immigrant child being hampered by problems of communication and differing traditions is relatively powerless to offer any challenge to the opinion the teacher has formed of him, be it over or under favourable. Given objective assessment, the teacher is then in a position of knowing how much progress to expect from particular children and is in a position to fulfil his responsibility of providing the right amount of stimulation to their learning process. Moreover, the teacher and psychologist would then be able to provide a more reliable answer to the question of which immigrant children, if any, would be better placed in a special school or remedial class.

Our attention has recently been drawn to the need for valid

assessments of the abilities of immigrant pupils by an unpublished report by the ILEA mentioned in *The Times* of 19 December 1969. There appears to be evidence that the numbers of immigrant children being admitted to special schools for the educationally subnormal is on the increase, but the criteria for transferring these children is likely to be haphazard and, as we have seen, based on a restricted sample of their mental functioning. One cannot help wondering therefore if some of these children are really in the right schools. If they are inappropriately placed this could have a crucial bearing on their achievements throughout life.

9.   The present investigation

We have seen that there is evidence from many different sources of the need to reflect upon the methods we use to assess the abilities of immigrant and indeed any of our disadvantaged children. In posing a particular problem immigrant children are serving to highlight neglected weaknesses in our traditional methods of psychological assessment and are causing us to pause and have many second thoughts.

After reviewing the lines of approach which have been made in the past, it seemed that there was a case for devising tests in which the assessment would be made on the basis of how well the children learn, and in particular how they learn to do the kinds of task which will be necessary for them to make progress in school. The scores on such tests would be likely to have a closer relationship to future educational progress if they had a verbal content, but whether verbal or non-verbal they can never be culture-free so that separate norms would be needed for the different cultural groups.

A basic difficulty in constructing such tests would be to ensure that the content of the tests would be unfamiliar for all the children so that no matter how many years they have been at school in this country they would still have to learn the tests; the type of learning task involved would also have to be closely related to the kind of mental processes involved in making progress with learning in school; and the tests would have to be such that even the slowest and lingusitically most handicapped child would be able to reveal his actual learning ability.

A battery of five tests was devised according to these considerations. A brief description of the tests developed and used in the course of this research may be found in Chapter Three and fuller details of the tests and the procedure for their administration are given in Appendix Four.

CHAPTER TWO

Aims and Outline of the Research

1. Aims

The principle aim of this research has been to devise tests of learning ability which can be used to assess the abilities of children with all degrees of linguistic and other cultural handicaps.

In the process of evaluating the tests with a particular sample of immigrant children, it was necessary to take account of other factors in the children, their school and home surroundings which were likely to have an important bearing on their achievements in school. By relating this information to the actual progress made by these immigrant children, it was hoped that this research would also throw some light on the factors which will promote their adjustment to school and further development of their abilities.

2. Design of the research

A battery of five individually administered learning tests was constructed and administered to a sample of Indian children during their first year at junior school and to a sample of English children of comparable age. The children were also assessed on various individual tests of intelligence so that it would be possible to investigate the relative validity of the two types of test in predicting achievement in school. Estimates of each child's ability were obtained from the class teachers and these, together with the experimental learning tests and intelligence tests, were validated against measures of attainment obtained at the end of the children's second year in the junior school.

Information concerning the other variables was obtained from the teachers and children through interviews and by the use of various questionnaires and rating scales. It was possible to analyse statistically the effects of 24 pupil variables and four variables to do with the teachers and schools.

The learning ability tests will be described in detail in the next chapter. Other instruments used in the research, outlined later in the present chapter, may be found in an unpublished thesis by the present writer (Haynes 1970).

3. Selection of the samples

In selecting the samples, consideration had to be given to the time which would be entailed in administering the learning, intelligence and attainment tests individually. Approximately three hours would be needed for each child and for the most part only the present writer would be available for carrying out the testing and collecting the rest of the personal and background data. It would have been desirable to try out the tests with children from various cultural backgrounds and from different age groups, but the sample of children would not be large enough to permit such a wide range and it was decided to select the immigrant children from one cultural group and to select a smaller sample of English children, both samples being drawn from the same one-year age group. By including a sample of English children, it would be possible to see whether the learning ability tests would add to our traditional methods of assessment in their case also, and with the two samples cover a wide range of Western acculturation.

A sample of Indian children was selected for the study. This choice was made for two main reasons: all the children's parents were from a homogeneous linguistic, religious, economic and geographical background, namely, Punjabi-speaking Sikhs; and there is a high concentration of these children in an area accessible from the point of view of carrying out the research. In fact, all the children, both Indian and English, who took part in this research were resident in the Southall district of the London Borough of Ealing.

The tests themselves are suitable for a wide age range, possibly from six to thirteen years, but in view of the foregoing practical considerations of time available for testing it was necessary to restrict the sample to one year group. Since it is important to diagnose learning problems as early as possible, it was decided to start at the younger end of the scale. By seven years most children can be expected to respond to some test material and so the first year age group of the junior school, seven- to eight-year-olds, was selected as the most appropriate group with which to begin.

The class teachers were asked to rate all the Indian and English children in the seven-plus age group who were resident in Southall on a five-point scale of general ability. The distributions of ability were calculated for the Indian and English children separately and the selection of the samples was made at random within each ability group in such a way that the distributions of ability for the total number of Indian and English children in the age group were proportionately represented (see Table 2). The random samples were

30

adjusted for control on sex (see Table 3), for proportionate representation across schools, and in the case of the Indian children for a third variable, namely length of schooling in England (see Table 4). The adjustment of the samples was effected by rejecting the last children selected at random and re-selecting at random from a group with the specified characteristics. The distribution of ability in the finally selected sample was kept as near as possible to the distribution of the parent sample.

TABLE 2: *Indian and English samples. Distribution of ability according to teacher ratings in the available and selected samples*

	INDIAN SAMPLE		ENGLISH SAMPLE	
ABILITY GROUP	CHILDREN AVAILABLE N=217	SELECTED SAMPLE N=125	CHILDREN AVAILABLE N=416	SELECTED SAMPLE N=40
	Percentages			
1. Well below average. Dull and definitely backward	3	4	5	5
2. Below Average	22	24	23	22
3. Average	45	44	34	33
4. Above Average	23	19	20	20
5. Well above average. Certain of a grammar school place or equivalent ability level	7	9	18	20

TABLE 3: *Indian and English samples. Distribution of sex in available and selected samples*

	INDIAN SAMPLE N=125		ENGLISH SAMPLE N=40	
	CHILDREN AVAILABLE	SELECTED SAMPLE	CHILDREN AVAILABLE	SELECTED SAMPLE
Boys	50%	52%	53%	52·5%
Girls	50%	48%	47%	47·5%

TABLE 4: *Indian sample. Length of previous education in England*

YEARS AT SCHOOL	CHILDREN AVAILABLE N=217	SELECTED SAMPLE N=125
0 None	18%	14%
1 1 year or less	14%	10%
2 1–2 years	31%	29%
3 More than 2 years	37%	47%

The English children were drawn from each of the nine junior schools in the Southall area. The Indian children were also drawn from four 'dispersal' schools outside the Southall area, to which transport was being provided for some Indian children resident in Southall. Three children moved to different schools in the neighbouring boroughs during the course of the research and were followed up there. Seven Indian children left the area and could not be traced, so that the final follow-up was completed on 118 Indians only.

4. Pupil variables

(a) Information obtained from the children

The children themselves provided direct information concerning their abilities, their attitude to school, and the influence of linguistic and other factors in their home background.

Information concerning abilities was obtained through their scores on intelligence, attainment and the learning ability tests. The test programme was arranged to spread over three of four sessions of $\frac{1}{2}$ to $\frac{3}{4}$ hour each.

At the end of these test sessions, the psychologist rated the children on three attributes of their behaviour as revealed during the test situation: confidence, concentration and co-operation.

In the second year of the study the children were interviewed individually in order to obtain information about their family backgrounds, their allegiance to Indian traditions, and their integration with non-Indian children. A questionnaire was specially constructed and was used as a basis for these interviews, but the questions became part of a general conversation with the child so that they were often phrased less formally and asked in a different and

more spontaneous order. The scoring and analysis of this questionnaire will be described in Chapter Five.

During the second year the children were also given a questionnaire
to complete themselves concerning their attitudes to school, the
Pupil's School Questionnaire. This questionnaire which consists of
10 attitude scales was specially developed to measure junior school
children's attitudes (Barker Lunn J. C. 1969) and was administered
to the children in small groups. Help in understanding the questions
was given where necessary.

At the end of the second year the children were again tested with
the same tests of attainment, namely the English Picture Vocabulary
Test and the vocabulary sub-test of the Wechsler Intelligence Scale
for Children, the Holborn and Schonell reading tests and the
Staffordshire Arithmetic Test. Their raw scores on these tests
constitute the chief criterion for the validity of the learning ability
tests.

(*i*) *Selection of the tests of intelligence and attainment.* In addition
to the tests of learning ability, the Indian and English children
were given a battery of intelligence and attainment tests: the Performance Scale and the vocabulary sub-test of the Verbal Scale of the
Wechsler Intelligence Scale for Children, the English Picture
Vocabulary Test; the Goodenough Draw-a-Man Test; the Schonell
Reading Test; the Holborn Reading Scale together with the comprehension questions and the Staffordshire Arithmetic Test. All these
tests are designed to be administered in an individual test situation.
Apart from this consideration the reasons for selecting these particular tests were as follows:

(*ii*) *The Wechsler Intelligence Scale for Children* (*Wechsler, D. 1949*).
This test was chosen because of its wide usage by educational
psychologists in assessing the ability of children of this age, and
this test rather than the Terman-Merrill was chosen on account of it
having a separate scale of non-verbal items. Owing to the language
handicaps of the Indian children, it would have been quite meaningless to give them verbal tests of intelligence or indeed group tests of
any kind.

The vocabulary sub-test from the Verbal Scale was used, however,
not as a measure of intelligence but as a means of assessing the
child's understanding of English. This test like the other attainment
tests was given during the child's first year in the junior school and at
the end of his second year at the school. The administration and
scoring of the vocabulary test was just as stringent for the Indian
as the English children.

On the Performance Scale, on the other hand, it was felt that the Indian children would achieve more valid scores if extra demonstration items could be made available[1]. The raw scores of the Wechsler sub-tests were used in the analysis as well as the Performance Scale IQ, which is computed from the standardized scores on the sub-tests.

(*iii*) *Goodenough's Draw-a-Man Test* (*Goodenough, F. L. and Harris, D. B. 1963*). It was decided to include this much-used and so-called culture-free test so as to obtain more information about the validity of this type of test in making educational assessments. The children were all asked to draw a man, the emphasis being on the word 'man'. If the child drew a woman (which did happen in nine cases) this was scored and the child was not asked to make a second drawing.

The scoring procedure outlined in the Harris (1963) revision of the Goodenough scale was followed. Because of the element of subjectivity which comes into the scoring of this test, the children's drawings were scored independently by two educational psychologists (one being the present writer) and any differences in assessment were resolved through discussions and comparison with other drawings.

(*iv*) *The English Picture Vocabulary Test:* (*Brimer, M. A. and Dunn, L. M. 1963*). This test was included in the battery since it was foreseen that many of the Indian children who would not manage to score on the Wechsler vocabulary sub-test would find this test considerably less demanding and it would be more discriminating among the children with a greater degree of language handicap.

Test 1 (age range 5·0–8·11) of the English Picture Vocabulary Test was given at the initial testing and at the final testing with the Indian children, and Test 2 (age range 7·0–11·11) was given at the

---

[1] Two extra demonstration items were used on the Picture Completion in the manner outlined by Murphy (1957) in the case of five children. With this additional opportunity for demonstrating the task involved in the Picture Completion sub-test it may be said that all the children had understood what they had to do. The same cannot be said, however, for the Picture Arrangement and Block Design sub-tests. On the Picture Arrangement, the first three items presented no special difficulty with the Indian children, but when it came to item D and the remaining items it was difficult to get across the idea that the pictures now had to be arranged so that they would tell a story. All the examiner could do was to emphasize the word 'story', but there is no doubt that some of the Indian children were still prevented by language difficulty from achieving higher scores. On the Block Design a difficulty which sometimes occurs with the English children, namely the tendency to copy the sides as well as the tops of the examiner's demonstration models, was more marked with the Indian children. No special difficulty was encountered with the Object Assembly or the Coding sub-test.

final testing of the English children. It was not possible to use Test 2 with the Indian children since it would have been too difficult for many of them. Raw scores only were used in the analysis.

(*v*) *Schonell Graded Reading Vocabulary Test: (Schonell, F. J. 1951).* This particular test was chosen on account of its wide range and particularly on account of its discriminatory value at the lower levels of reading ability. Reading ages are given from 5 to 15 years, but for the purpose of this study the raw scores were used in the analysis and they were not converted into reading ages. The test was administered in the way outlined by Schonell (1951).

(*vi*) *The Holborn Reading Scale: (Watts, A. F. 1948).* This test was also administered and scored according to the method outlined in the manual. The test was included for two reasons: (1) to obtain a more complete assessment of the child's accuracy in reading, and (2) because the test includes comprehension questions and in the case of immigrant children it is essential to know how much they can understand of what they read.

Each child received two scores on this test—one for accuracy and one for comprehension. The reading ages for accuracy can range on this test from 5 years 9 months to 13 years 9 months, although raw scores only were used for this analysis.

(*vii*) *The Staffordshire Arithmetic Test (Hebron, M. E. 1958).* This test was selected on account of its wide age range and, like the other tests of attainment, was included in this battery for its discriminatory value at the lower levels of ability.

The test yields arithmetic ages between 5 years 8 months and 15 years 6 months, whereas the other widely used tests such as the Schonell and Kelvin have a basal age of 7 years and would have proved too difficult for many of the immigrant children.

An additional advantage of the Staffordshire Test is that the first items involve the child in recording in writing numbers spoken by the examiner. This item is particularly relevant for immigrant children with their difficulty in verbal recognition and understanding.

The other items in the test involve the mechanical application of the four basic rules. A test involving problem sums would obviously have a high language content and, in the case of children with language difficulties, might not add very much to measures of vocabulary and reading ability.

(*b*) *Information Obtained from the Teachers*

An attempt was made to control for the effects of other important personal variables, such as the child's previous education, the regularity of his current attendance at school, his general health, his attitude to school work, his integration with English children and his emotional adjustment.

The information was obtained from the teachers either by direct questions or scales for rating various attributes of the child. The questions and rating scales were compiled into one questionnaire, which class teachers completed during the first and second years of the study. This information was therefore obtained twice in respect of each child. The scoring and analysis of the questionnaire will be discussed in Chapter Five.

5. School, class and teacher variables

Numerous aspects of the child's school, class and teacher are also known to be highly relevant to a child's progress, and information was collected about many aspects of the amenities and procedures in the schools and classes concerned, such as, for example, the numbers of children in the class with language difficulties and the class teacher's native tongue.

Much of this information did not prove feasible for statistical analysis owing to the small sample and skewed distribution of these variables. Nevertheless, some information was obtained which could be subjected to further analysis and this will be discussed fully in Chapter Five.

The information was obtained by two questionnaires, which were drawn up for the purposes of this study and formed the basis of semi-structured interviews with the teachers.

A third questionnaire, Teachers' Opinions about Indian children (see Appendix One), is an attitude scale specially constructed for this research, and as its name suggests is designed to obtain information about teachers' feelings about Indian children, another variable which was thought likely to have an important bearing on the child's progress.

A copy of the statements in this questionnaire is to be found in Appendix One. It will be seen that it consists of statements about Indian children with which the teacher is asked to indicate the degree of his agreement or disagreement. An outline of the method used to construct this scale is also given in Appendix One.

CHAPTER THREE

The Learning Ability Tests

THE main objective of this research is to develop a variety of tasks with which the child's ability to learn can be measured directly in a standardized test situation. In doing so, the following principal considerations were kept in mind:

(1)   the tests should not assume any prior knowledge of English, so that every child no matter how severe his linguistic handicap could understand what is required of him;

(2)   the tests must be designed so that the child gives objective evidence that he has understood the instructions. The tests must therefore be sufficiently easy to begin with so as to ensure that such a response could be made;

(3)   the tests must require learning on the part of all the children regardless of their ability or length of schooling in this country;

(4)   the tests must cover a wide enough range to be discriminating throughout the seven- to eight-year age group and possibly a wider age group;

(5)   the tests must sample a wide variety of the skills which are called upon in learning situations in school.

1.   Discovering suitable content and presentation of the tests

In planning the project, thought was given to the possibility of modifying existing group tests of ability such as the NFER Non-Verbal Test, the Moray House Picture Test, Raven's Matrices, Porteus Mazes or Dr. Ortar's tests by introducing a period of coaching before re-testing on the same test and taking final scores as the predictors. Such tests it was thought might be a useful screening device which would be used by teachers. This idea was abandoned, however, for several reasons:

(a)   the difficulty in getting across the instructions;

(b)   the inability of some children to write or draw a response;

(c) for the coaching to be of any value, it must be geared to individual needs (Mackay, and Vernon 1963);

(d) the data produced by Lloyd and Pidgeon (1961) showing that Indian children were unable to benefit from coaching on group tests;

(e) the relatively poor predictive value of non-verbal tests;

(f) the impossibility of giving group verbal tests owing to language difficulties.

The possibility of adapting existing individual intelligence tests into learning situations was then considered and various ideas were tried out with small samples of immigrant children of junior school age. For example, items from the Nebraska and Snijders-Ooman Tests for deaf children were tried, incorporating a period of demonstration with failed items before re-testing. The same procedure was tried out with the Grace Arthur Stencil Design Kit, Kohs Blocks, Porteus Mazes, Goodenough's Draw-a-Man Test, and the test of geometric form learning used by Mackay (1962).

It became clear, however, that the children quickly became bored in this kind of learning situation in which they are merely required to observe passively the further demonstrations. It appeared essential that the tests should require the child to be an active participant at all stages. This is particularly vital in a situation where verbal communication is already minimal and the only contribution the child can make is through some alternative form of behaviour. Again, informal sampling techniques with immigrant children of different ages were used to try out provisional test material.

2.   Rationale behind the type of task selected for the learning tests

A survey of the literature dealing with experimental studies of human learning did not reveal any well defined factors of learning which could be used as guidelines for constructing these tests of learning ability.

The research which has been reviewed in detail by Guilford (1967) indicates that there is no general learning ability common to all types of task. Many learning factors have been identified which are closely related to the specific task and conditions of learning and it must be concluded that a test of learning ability involves several component abilities, only some of which will be shared with other learning tasks and tests of ability.

Woodrow's (1946) review had earlier pointed to the evidence of more than one learning factor which have ambiguous relationships with each other and to ability factors and Jensen (1961) has also

38

established the discrepant relationship between ability to learn and measured intelligence as a result of which he has put forward the hypothesis of two types of learning ability: basic learning ability or associative learning and conceptual learning ability, the latter being more highly related to performance on intelligence tests and achievement in school.

Although there is no direct evidence that tests of learning add to the predictions of school learning made by general or verbal ability tests, it seems that this may be accounted for by the artificiality of the learning tasks which have generally been used in the past and the notorious unreliability of gain scores which have so often been used as measures of learning in these researches. Mackay and Vernon (1963), in a study involving 36 primary school children aged 8-9 and 10-11 years, devised and administered a battery of nine group tests of more complex and meaningful learning and found that these were significantly related to subsequent school learning, but only if the final performance reached on the tests rather than the gain scores were used.

In devising the present battery, an effort was made to construct the tests along ability dimensions which would have relevance to school learning—the major difficulty here being to avoid making them too close to school learning or the transfer effects from the previous learning would become too great and preclude the child from revealing the extent of his ability for new learning.

3. Brief description of the tests

There is no doubt that the most important learning task which faces the immigrant child is learning a new language. How well he can do this is bound to have a profound effect on every aspect of his progress in school, be it social or academic, and the first two tests are concerned with the child's verbal learning ability.

The first of these, *Verbal Learning 1. Objects,* requires the child to learn verbal material which hitherto has been quite meaningless to him in the form of learning unfamiliar names of some quite common everyday objects. A second test of verbal learning, *Verbal Learning 2. Syllables,* was also designed. This task involves the serial rote learning of nonsense syllables. The reason for including this test was to see if the child's skill in a more repetitive kind of learning gives a better indication of how he is likely to fare in his school work than the first more meaningful type of learning. At first, one might hope that there would be a more positive relationship between the learning on the first test and the child's subsequent attainment, but the second less attractive task demands far more drive and persistence on the part of the child and these are vital requirements when it comes to persevering with school work.

The third test, *Analogies,* is much more concerned with the child's reasoning ability. The material devised for this is a set of thirteen analogies of increasing difficulty in the form of geometric figures. The child has to complete the missing items, making the appropriate drawing himself. If he draws an incorrect figure or does not know how to proceed, further examples of the analogy are shown giving him further clues as to the principles involved and he is then given a further opportunity to complete the original items and improve on his initial performance. By introducing the idea that the child has to create his own illustrations, one can be certain that he really has understood and formulated the nature of the problem involved. All the figures which have to be drawn are within the drawing capabilities of children of this age. However, the scoring is not based on the child's skill in drawing but on his grasp of the nature of the drawing which is required.

The fourth test, *Concept Formation,* is one in which the child is required to classify sets of objects according to their various perceptual attributes. The sets of objects increase in perceptual complexity and, by requiring him to switch from one classificatory principle to another, a situation is provided in which it is possible to assess the flexibility of the child's thought processes. A record is kept of how much help the child has required in attaining a particular concept and with each set of material he has an opportunity for demonstrating what he has learned on the previous items.

Lovell (1955), in his investigation into the nature of intellectual deterioration in adolescents and young adults, presents strong evidence that there is an ability to group ideas or objects to a criterion and switch from one criterion to another not adequately measured by tests of general, verbal or spatial ability. The view that concept formation is inadequately measured by the usual items in intelligence tests has been expressed by several other writers, notably Hearnshaw (1951) and Annett (1959), indicating the importance of this aspect of learning and the need for further studies.

It was felt that the battery of learning tests would not be complete without some assessment of the child's ability to acquire an understanding of numerical concepts and the *Number Series* test was devised for this purpose. The number series item which involves an appreciation of quantity and the relationships between quantities has been a much used item in general intelligence tests. It was decided to use the similar test items, only with concrete materials rather than figures which the child has to make up to the appropriate amounts. This, like the creative drawing response in the Analogies test, means that for the child to make a correct response he must really understand what is involved and is not passively selecting one out of several possible answers already supplied. Again, a teaching situation is built into the test procedure enabling the child to respond more fully to the test material.

The ability to remember is undoubtedly of fundamental importance in the child's capacity not only to retain particular information but to benefit from previous experience in a more general way. Memory is involved in all the tests in this battery, but always in conjunction with other mental skills. In particular, a long-term test of recall was incorporated into the tests of verbal learning.

It was felt that a more specific measure of immediate memory would enhance the assessment of these children. Again, owing to their language difficulties, a non-verbal situation had to be used for the *Memory* test and for this purpose a situation somewhat similar to a form of 'Kim's Game' was devised. This test proved to be extremely unreliable, however, and was discarded from the validation analysis.

The final form and content of each test was achieved after several types of item had been tried out, and after many changes had been made in the presentation of the tests. In order to mobilize the child's co-operation and motivation and convey the instructions, a test situation was created in which the relationship became one of helper and one being helped rather than examiner and examinee. A standardized procedure has been formulated so that the same amount of help could be given by different testers. A more detailed description of the tests, the method of administration and scoring procedures, may be found in Appendix Four.

4. The reliability of the learning tests

The reliability coefficients of the learning ability tests are derived from scores obtained by the test-retest technique. This means that the same tests were performed by the same children at two different times and the correlation computed between the first and second set of test scores.

Owing to difficulties in controlling conditions which influence scores on a retest, the test-retest method is generally less useful than the other methods of estimating the reliability of a test, namely the split-half technique and the method of giving a parallel form of the test. The use of these latter methods was precluded, however, by the impracticability of dividing these particular tests into two equivalent halves and by the unavailability of alternative forms of the tests.

When using the test-retest method, a sufficient time interval must be allowed between the first and second administration of the test to offset immediate memory effects as far as possible, and this it has been possible to do. On the other hand, the time interval must not be so long for the growth changes to affect the test scores.

In order to estimate the reliabilities of these learning tests two retest samples were selected: (1) 25 children with a 14-week time interval between the two administrations of the tests, and (2) 25 children with a 21-week time interval between the tests. It was necessary to have the two different time intervals on account of the length of time it took to administer the tests, making it impossible to re-administer the tests to a sufficient number of children after the same interval of time.

The samples were approximately representative of the total sample of Indian children with regard to distribution of ability as had been estimated by the teachers and with regard to the length of their previous schooling. It was not possible to select the samples with exactly equivalent distributions on these characteristics and at the same time comply to the standard test-retest time intervals, and so to some extent the samples had to be selected on a judgement basis. The samples were similar with regard to having one school holiday period in the interval between the tests and with regard to being representative by sex distribution on the total available sample. It was not possible to calculate the reliabilities for the two samples separately owing to the small size of the samples but no significant correlations had been found between date of birth, date of testing and performance on the learning tests (see Table A2.1 Correlation Matrix of Pupil Variables 1. Indian sample), which indicates that for this particular sample factors of maturation were not giving rise to any important source of variance in the initial test scores.[1]

---

[1] In deciding upon a formula for calculating the reliability coefficients it was assumed that although the test-retest correlations within the two samples would be similar, the deviations from an overall mean might be distorted because of the different test-retest time intervals, and as a precaution the following formula was used:

$$r = \frac{\Sigma(x_1 - \bar{x}_1)(y_1 - \bar{y}_1) + \Sigma(x_2 - \bar{x}_2)(y_2 - \bar{y}_2)}{\sqrt{\{\Sigma(x_1 - \bar{x}_1)^2 + \Sigma(x_2 - \bar{x}_2)^2\} - \{\Sigma(y_1 - \bar{y}_1)^2 \times \Sigma(y_2 - \bar{y}_2)^2\}}}$$

Footnote continued on bottom of opposite page

The reliability coefficients may be found in Table 5 together with the standard errors for each of the tests. The standard error of measurement has the advantage of showing within what limits a score may be trusted; it indicates the margin at both sides of the score

TABLE 5: *Learning ability tests. Reliability coefficients and standard errors of measurement*

TEST	RELIABILITY COEFFICIENT	STANDARD ERROR
Verbal Learning Objects:		
1. Score on Learning Trials	0·75	5·98
2. Score on Retest	0·76	1·79
3. Score on Last Learning Trial	0·66	1·14
4. Score on First Retest Trial	0·73	0·92
Verbal Learning Syllables:		
1. Score on Learning Trials	0·77	4·81
2. Score on Retest	0·53	2·36
3. Score on Last Learning Trial	0·62	1·26
4. Score on First Retest Trial	0·47	1·17
Analogies:		
1. Initial Score	0·69	1·54
2. Final Score	0·72	1·54
3. Gain Score	0·23	1·11
Concept Formation:		
1. No. of Prompts	0·58	3·21
2. No. of Spontaneous Classifications	0·65	0·86
3. No. of Classifications on Set 6	0·39	0·67
Number Series:		
1. Completion of Series	0·77	1·53
2. Filling-in Series	0·55	0·82
3. Combined Score	0·64	0·74
Memory:		
1. Total Number remembered	0·35	1·58
2. Memory Span	−0·02	0·78

Where x_1 = score on first application of test: y_1 = score on retest.
$\bar{x}_1$ = mean score for sample 1 on first test: $\bar{y}_1$ = mean score for sample 1 on retest.
i = 1 refers to measures of retest sample 1.
i = 2 refers to measures of retest sample 2.
This is a modification of the formula for calculating product moment correlation coefficients (Garrett, 1958, p. 139) obtained by pooling within sample variances and co-variances of the scores.

which could be attributed to chance error. The smaller the standard error, the less allowance one needs to make for the unreliability of the score. It should be noted that the error of measurement varies with the size of the unit of measurement so that the standard errors of the tests in this battery are not directly comparable.

5. Selection of the scoring methods of the learning ability tests

Before embarking on the validation of the tests it was necessary to select the most reliable and discriminating of the scoring methods. A list of scoring methods is given in Table 5. On the basis of the reliabilities (Table 5), the inter-correlations of the test scores (Table A2.3) and the distribution of the test scores, the following decisions were reached:

a. *Verbal Learning Objects and Verbal Learning Syllables*

It was decided to take scores 1 and 2 (the total numbers of correct responses on the learning and retest trials) in the case of both tests because:

i. score 1 has maximum reliability (0·75 for Verbal Learning Objects and 0·77 for Verbal Learning Syllables);

ii. it would be advisable to retain the same methods for both tests, so that Score 4 (the number of correct responses on the first retest trial) was not selected since on the Verbal Learning Syllables this measure has a low reliability (0·47) and a poor distribution;

iii. score 3 (the number of correct responses on the last learning trial) was abandoned because it has a poor spread of scores and high association with the other verbal learning measures, the correlations with the other scoring methods ranging from 0·74 to 0·91 (Table A2.3);

iv. owing to the high correlations between the selected scoring methods (the correlation values range between 0·79 to 0·90) it was thought that at a later stage in the analysis one of these might also become redundant.

b. *Analogies*

Score 2, the Final Score (i.e. the number of correct responses achieved with the teaching examples), was selected because:

i. Initial Score and Final Scores are very highly correlated, ($r=0·92$) so that it would be unnecessary to retain both;

ii. although the Initial and Final Scores are approximately equally reliable, with reliability coefficients 0·69 and 0·72 respectively, the Final Score is marginally more so;

iii. the Gain Score is unreliable with a reliability coefficient of only 0·23;

iv. the Final Score makes more intuitive sense as it allows for the new learning which has taken place during the test to be included in the score.

c. Concept Formation

Scores 1 and 2 (the number of prompts given during the test and the number of spontaneous classifications achieved with the first five sets of material) were selected on the basis of the reliability coefficients which were 0·58 and 0·65 respectively and on account of:

i. the low reliability (0·39) of Score 3 and its poor distribution;

ii. the possibility of pooling Scores 2 and 3 was examined on a weighted and unweighted basis, but this decreased the reliability of score and in view of the poor distribution of Score 3 it was decided to reject this scoring method from further consideration.

d. Number Series

It was decided to combine Scores 1 and 2 (the total numbers of correct responses on the two parts of the test) on account of:

i. the reliabilities of the test scores. Score 2 on its own has a reliability of only 0·55 whereas the reliability of the scores on the two parts of the test combined is 0·64;

ii. the logical step of combining the two test scores since they are derived from items of the same type.

e. Memory

The decision to reject both scores and hence the test altogether was reached when considering the reliabilities, both of which were exceedingly low (0·35 and −0·2). A suggestion for a possible improvement in the method of administering this kind of test, which might then produce more reliable scores is discussed in the concluding chapter.

In order to give a complete record of this research and for possible relevance to future research work, it should be mentioned that an alternative method of scoring the Verbal Learning Tests was investigated. The measure was based on the number of trials it took for the child to learn a specified number of objects or syllables to (a) a criterion of 2 correct responses in one of the eight learning trials and (b) to a criterion of 50 per cent correct responses in one trial. In view of the U-shaped distributions of these scores, however, there seemed little point in subjecting the scores to further analysis, except in the case of Verbal Learning Syllables to a criterion of 2 correct syllables, since the distribution of scores approached the characteristics of a normal curve distribution. In this case the scoring method correlated at 0·81 with scoring method 1 and at 0·71 with scoring method 2. Since these coefficients are of the same order as the inter-correlations of the two Verbal Learning Scores already selected (0·79 to 0·90), it was decided not to consider this scoring method further.

6. Selected scoring methods

The selected methods of scoring the learning ability tests together with the abbreviations to be used subsequently in the test are as follows:

Verbal Learning Objects:	Score 1. Score on learning trials	(VLO 1)
	Score 2. Score on retest trials	(VLO 2)
Verbal Learning Syllables:	Score 1. Score on learning trials	(VLS 1)
	Score 2. Score on retest trials	(VLS 2)
Analogies:	Score 2. Final Score	(ANALOG)
Concept Formation:	Score 1. Number of prompts	(CON 1)
	Score 2. Number of spontaneous classifications	(CON 2)
Number Series:	Score 3. Combined scores 1 and 2	(NOS)

CHAPTER FOUR

The Validity of the Learning Ability Tests

THE statistical analysis to be described in the present chapter falls into four main sections:

1. the validation of the learning ability tests against (a) concurrent and (b) predictive criteria with respect to the Indian children;

2. the validation of the tests against predictive data obtained from the English children;

3. a comparative analysis of (a) the Indian and English children and (b) the Indian boys and Indian girls on the learning ability, intelligence and attainment tests;

4. an examination of the validity of the teachers' estimates of ability in the case of the Indian and English children.

The analysis of the educational achievements of the Indian children in relation to factors within their home and school surroundings and in relation to other pupil variables will be presented in the next chapter.

1. Concurrent and predictive validity (Indian children)

Using the selected scoring methods, information concerning the validity of the learning ability tests was obtained from:

(a) correlations between scores on the learning tests, intelligence tests and teachers' estimates of ability (concurrent validity);

(b) correlations between the scores on the learning tests and the criterion tests (predictive ability);

(c) principal components analysis of the scores on the learning tests, intelligence tests and criterion tests (concurrent and predictive validity);

(d) regression analysis of four of the criterion measures on the selected learning test scores, the intelligence test scores and the teachers' estimates of ability (predictive validity);

47

(e) correlations between learning test scores and rates of progress in the case of children who had zero scores on the initial testing of attainments (predictive validity).

(a) *Correlations Between Learning and Intelligence Tests and Teachers' Estimates of Ability*

Product moment correlations were computed for the 21 variables: i.e. eight learning test scores, seven intelligence test scores and six criterion test scores. These are to be found in Table A2.1 together with the inter-correlation coefficients of the other pupil variables.

i. *Correlations with intelligence tests.* The correlations between the batteries of intelligence and learning tests are not readily summarized. Although there is some association between the two types of test, it is clear that this is not consistently close since many of the correlations, though positive, are low. The Draw-a-Man Test in particular shows consistently low correlations with the learning tests as well as with the criterion measures.

There are, however, significant relationships between WISC Picture Completion and WISC Performance Scale IQ and all the learning ability tests (at the one per cent level between WISC Performance Scale IQ and CON 2 and VLO2 and at the 0·1 per cent level in all other cases) and a significant relationship (0·1 per cent level) between WISC Block Design and the Number Series Test.

Evidence for the validity of the Number Series and Analogies Tests comes from correlational analysis of the sample of English children where significant (0·1 per cent level) correlation coefficients are found between these tests and the WISC Performance Scale Sub-tests other than Coding (Table A2.2).

A principal components analysis of these test scores to be discussed later in the chapter brings out the relationship between the two types of test more clearly as well as their different associations with the criterion tests.

ii. *Correlations with teachers' estimates of ability.* The correlations between scores on the tests of learning ability and the teachers' estimates of ability made during the children's first term at junior school are also to be found in the correlation matrix of pupil variables for the Indian Sample (Table A2.1).

The correlations with the eight learning test scores range from 0·24 for CON 1 to 0·38 in the case of VLS 1. The correlations of the teachers' ratings of general ability summed over the subsequent two years (variable 45 in the same matrix) with the learning test scores range from 0·30 in the case of CON 1 to 0·53 in the case of the NOS test.

All these correlation coefficients are significant at the 0·1 per cent level and provide an important source of evidence for the concurrent validity of the tests.

(b) *Correlations Between Scores on the Tests of Learning Ability and Criterion Tests*

The sample of Indian children used in all the statistical analyses involving the criterion scores was reduced in size from the original 125 to 118 since seven of the children assessed with the learning tests had moved out of the area and could not be traced for the assessments on the criterion tests.

The correlations between these two sets of scores are listed in Table 6 and in all cases reveal a significant (0·1 per cent level) association between the two sets of tests.

Further support for the predictive validity of the learning ability tests was derived from the principal components analysis and the regression analysis to be described in following sections of the present chapter. Further details of the principal components analysis are to be found in Appendix Three.

TABLE 6: *Correlations of the learning ability test scores with the criterion test scores*

(Indian Sample N = 118)

	SCHONELL RA	HOLBORN RA	HOLBORN COMPRE-HENSION	ENGLISH PICTURE VOCAB.	WISC VOCAB.	STAFFORD-SHIRE ARITHMETIC
VLO 1	0·68	0·67	0·65	0·55	0·49	0·41
VLO 2	0·61	0·60	0·59	0·50	0·46	0·33
VLS 1	0·61	0·62	0·62	0·44	0·46	0·46
VLS 2	0·60	0·62	0·58	0·39	0·41	0·44
ANALOG	0·35	0·35	0·42	0·40	0·44	0·54
CON 1	0·28	0·29	0·36	0·35	0·32	0·37
CON 2	0·27	0·26	0·38	0·39	0·33	0·40
NOS	0·41	0·41	0·47	0·44	0·46	0·57

(c) *Principal Components Analysis of the Scores on the Learning Tests, Intelligence Tests and Criterion Tests*

It should be pointed out that the Draw-a-Man Test was not included in this factor analysis on account of the very low correlations between this test and the learning tests and the criterion measures for both the Indian and English children (see Appendix Two).

The computer extracted four principal components from the 20 sets of test scores being investigated. Together these accounted for 69·5 per cent of the variance in the criterion scores (see Table A2.4). An oblique rotated solution was computed by the Promax procedure and the factor loadings are given in Table 7 and the inter-correlations of the factors in Table A2.5. The four factors which have been derived from this may be described as follows:

Factor 1. Connecting the Verbal Learning tests with all the criteria, and with the reading and vocabulary tests in particular.

Factor 2. A different connection between Analogies, Concepts 1 and 2, Number Series and all the criteria. This factor possibly indicates a factor of general learning ability.

Both factors 1 and 2 link quite strongly with the criteria and confirm a split between the verbal and non-verbal learning tests which was already apparent from a preliminary principal components analysis of the learning tests on their own (see Table A2.7) in which the two components extracted are readily identified as a verbal factor and a non-verbal factor.

Factor 3. A connection between the intelligence measures, other than WISC Block Design, and the criteria other than Staffordshire Arithmetic. (WISC Block Design and Staffordshire Arithmetic are quite highly correlated and appear together in Factor 4.)

Factor 4. A connection between Analogies, Number Series, WISC Block Design and Staffordshire Arithmetic perhaps indicating an arithmetical/logical learning factor.

The first two factors to be extracted provide evidence of a closer connection between scores on the learning tests and criterion tests than between the intelligence and criterion tests and this was confirmed by the subsequent regression analysis.

(d) *Regression Analysis of the Criterion Scores on the Learning Ability Tests, Intelligence Tests and Teachers' Estimates of Ability*

Regression analysis is a statistical technique which shows the degree of relationship between two sets of scores. It indicates how closely the values of one of the variables can be estimated from the scores on the other variable. In this investigation more than two sets of scores were involved so that the particular method of stepwise linear regression was used to show which combination of the original measures would give the best estimate of performance on the criterion tests (the attainment tests at the end of the second year in the junior school). At each step the computer selects the variable which makes the largest reduction in the remainder of the variance in

TABLE 7: *Oblique primary factor loadings and communalities of eight learning test scores, intelligence tests and criterion scores*

VARIABLE	OBLIQUE PRIMARY FACTORS				COMMUNA-LITIES
	1	2	3	4	5
Intelligence Sub-tests:					
WISC Picture Completion	0·50	0·57	0·64	0·15	0·49
WISC Picture Arrangement	0·35	0·46	0·68	0·00	0·48
WISC Block Design	0·20	0·32	0·33	0·81	0·71
WISC Object Assembly	0·19	0·28	0·65	0·40	0·58
WISC Coding	0·19	0·04	0·62	−0·04	0·52
WISC Performance IQ	0·44	0·48	0·90	0·42	0·93
Learning Sub-tests:					
Analogies	0·37	0·65	0·37	0·52	0·59
Verbal Learning Objects 1	0·88	0·33	0·36	0·11	0·80
Verbal Learning Objects 2	0·83	0·27	0·31	0·10	0·73
Verbal Learning Syllables 1	0·83	0·28	0·32	0·23	0·77
Verbal Learning Syllables 2	0·80	0·24	0·36	0·23	0·73
Concept 1	0·25	0·81	0·27	0·25	0·74
Concept 2	0·26	0·80	0·32	0·22	0·70
Number Series	0·44	0·63	0·48	0·63	0·70
Criteria:					
Schonell Reading Age	0·88	0·60	0·52	−0·05	0·82
Holborn Reading Age	0·88	0·60	0·55	−0·07	0·84
Holborn Comprehension	0·87	0·69	0·59	0·00	0·85
Staffordshire Arithmetic	0·57	0·59	0·43	0·47	0·58
Picture Vocabulary	0·69	0·68	0·70	0·02	0·69
WISC Vocabulary	0·69	0·68	0·66	0·03	0·66

the criterion test. In each case the computer programme stopped when no further variable made a statistically significant (5 per cent) contribution to the regression and this is why the number of steps varies within the table (Table A2.7). An account of Stepwise Regression Analysis may be found in Applied Regression Analysis (Draper and Smith, 1966).

Three series of stepwise regressions were carried out. These are denoted A, B and C in the table (Table A2.7) and in the text.

Regression A. The first regression analysis involved the criterion measures and all the independent variables, i.e. the five learning tests, the seven intelligence test scores (this time, the Draw-a-Man Test was included) and the teachers' estimates of the child's ability. This regression was carried out to see which of all the original scores has the closest association with the criterion in question and which is the best combination of tests out of the entire battery.

Regression B. The second regression analysis used the criterion scores, the learning test scores and teachers' estimate.

Regression C. The third regression analysis used the criterion scores, the intelligence test scores and teachers' estimate.

Regression B and C give further information about the relationship between the sub-tests of the learning and intelligence test batteries and the criterion tests and provide a means of comparing their relative efficiency in forecasting performance on the criterion tests.

For the purposes of economy in time and cost five learning test scores and four criterion scores were selected for the regression analysis. They were selected as being representative of the complete test battery and the scores retained were as follows:

1. Verbal Learning Objects Score 1
2. Verbal Learning Syllables Score 1
3. Analogies
4. Concept Formation Score 2
5. Number Series

The criterion scores retained were:
1. Holborn Scale Reading Age
2. Holborn Scale Comprehension
3. English Picture Vocabulary Test
4. Staffordshire Arithmetic

A summary of the regressions is to be found in the statistical appendix (Table A2.7). Looking at each of the attainment test measures in turn the following conclusions were reached:

Holborn Scale Reading Age

A. One of the learning tests, Verbal Learning Objects, was selected first and this accounted for 44 per cent of the variance of the Holborn Scale Reading Age.

B.   The best combination of learning tests accounted for 51 per cent of the variance in the criterion. The teachers' estimate was not found to be making a significant addition to the learning tests in the prediction of this criterion.

C.   The best combination of the intelligence test scores, even with the teachers' estimate, only accounts for 29 per cent of the variance in the criterion.

Holborn Scale Comprehension

A.   Learning test scores were selected first and accounted for 57 per cent of the variance before any of the intelligence scores were selected.

B.   Regression B would have used the learning test scores and the teachers' estimate, but the results of regression A made the calculation of this regression redundant since learning tests had been selected by the computer in the first four steps of the first regression.

C.   Two intelligence test scores were selected, namely WISC Picture Completion and Picture Arrangement, but together with the teachers' estimate, they account for only 34 per cent of the variance.

Staffordshire Arithmetic

A.   Number Series were selected first together with other learning test scores and teachers' estimate account for 49 per cent of the variance.

B.   Regression B was omitted for the same reason as in the case of the Holborn Scale Comprehension, the learning test having already been selected in the first regression.

C.   The teachers' estimate was selected prior to any of the intelligence test scores. Together they only account for 35 per cent of the variance.

English Picture Vocabulary Scale

A.   One of the learning tests is shown to be the best prediction of subsequent attainment.

B.   The teachers' estimate is again conspicuous only by its absence and Verbal Learning Objects was selected first from amongst the learning tests.

C.   With the aid of the teachers' estimate, the intelligence test scores account for 40 per cent of the variance which is close to the 42 per cent accounted for by learning test scores. The learning tests and intelligence test scores are more balanced in forecasting this criterion, but the former still have a clear edge as regards their predictive value.

As a result of examining these three regression analyses it appeared that some of the variables either explained very little (as in the case of Analogies), or none at all (as in the case of WISC Block Design, WISC Coding and Draw-a-Man) of the variance in the criterion scores. However, a test may be valid even if it has not been picked out in the regression analysis. It may be overlapping in function with one of the other tests and before dismissing a test it should be considered in relation to the findings of the correlations and factor analysis.

Thus in the case of the WISC Block Design it can be seen from inspection of the correlation matrix in Table A2.1 that its highest correlation is 0·34 with the Staffordshire Arithmetic Test. This is significant at the 0·1 per cent level. These two tests also have high loadings on Factor 4 of the factor analysis of the initial test scores and criterion scores (Table 7) and these are indications that the WISC Block Design could be an efficient substitute as a predictor of arithmetic attainment for the Number Series and the teachers' estimate which were selected in the regression analyses (Table A2.7).

On the other hand WISC Coding and the Draw-a-Man Test both have low correlations with the criterion scores. It can be seen from Table A2.1 that these range from 0·15 to 0·29. But WISC Coding does have some link with the criterion scores since they have relatively high loading on Factor 3 of the factor analysis of the initial test scores and criterion scores (Table 7).

The two verbal learning tests, which overlapped in function to a certain extent, and the number series test appeared to be doing the most work in predicting educational achievement. To see if it were feasible to provide a valid but shorter version of the battery of learning tests a further regression analysis was carried out using Verbal Learning Objects Score 1 and Number Series only. The results for the four criteria examined are to be found in Table A2.8 and looking at each of the criterion tests in turn they may be summarized as follows:

Holborn Scale Reading Age

From inspection of Table A2.8 together with the previous re-gression results for the Holborn Scale Reading Age in Table A2.7, it will be seen that Verbal Learning Objects 1 and Number Series alone explained 49 per cent of the variance and Verbal Learning Objects 1 and Verbal Learning Syllables also explain 49 per cent of the variance. In other words the use of the Number Series test rather than

Verbal Learning Syllables will give an equally accurate prediction of Holborn Reading Age when combined with the Verbal Learning Objects.

Holborn Scale Comprehension

Verbal Learning Objects and Number Series were selected before Verbal Learning Syllables in the original regression (see Table A2.7 Regression A) so that their presence in this regression had already been noted. When Verbal Learning Syllables was selected at Step 3 it served to reduce the variance explained by Verbal Learning Objects, and further indicates the overlapping function of the two tests.

Staffordshire Arithmetic

From Table A2.7 it may be seen that Verbal Learning Objects was not selected in Regression A. In that case Number Series and the teachers' estimate accounted for 42 per cent of the variance whereas from this second regression it can be seen that Number Series and Verbal Learning Objects 1 account for 39 per cent.

English Picture Vocabulary

Verbal Learning Objects 1 and Number Series account for 38 per cent of the variance. In the first regression, Verbal Learning Syllables had not been selected, the best combination of the learning tests being Verbal Learning Objects 1, Number Series and Concept Formation which together accounted for 43 per cent of the variance.

In summary, it has been confirmed that:

(1) Verbal Learning Objects and Verbal Learning Syllables do overlap.

(2) Verbal Learning Objects and Number Series are a valid shorthand way of predicting the criteria, particularly with regard to the accuracy and comprehension of reading English.

(3) A wider combination of the learning and intelligence tests and the teachers' estimate, in the ways indicated by the first regression analysis, would yield a more valid instrument of prediction.

(e) *Correlations Between Learning Test Scores and Rates of Progress*

The validation of an intelligence or learning test against the criterion of rate of educational progress is normally precluded by the fact that the sample is not uniform in its initial attainments so that progress would be measured from a differing base line. As in the case of any gain score such a measure could be extremely unreliable and misleading. However, it is possible to select samples on the basis of their uniformity on some initial test score and investigate the relationships between their subsequent scores on the same test and their performance on another test. In the case of the sample of Indian children in the present research, it was possible to isolate two groups of children who had zero scores on two of the initial tests of attainments and then compute the correlations between their final scores on these tests and their scores on the tests of learning ability.

Sixteen children had zero scores on the Holborn Reading Scale and 31 children had zero scores on the Holborn Scale Comprehension test when they were first tested. The groups of zero scorers on the other tests of attainment were too small to be considered. Table A2.9 provides the correlation coefficients calculated for these samples together with their levels of significance. It will be seen from this table that all the learning tests correlate with progress in reading accuracy and comprehension and that the coefficients reach significance in the case of Verbal Learning Syllables.

2. Predictive validity (English children)

Evidence for the predictive validity of the learning ability tests was also obtained through correlational analysis of the scores of the English children on the learning tests and criterion scores (see Table A2.2). From this matrix it can be seen that there is a relatively poorer range of correlation coefficients between the intelligence test scores and the criterion scores (-0.05 to 0.49) than between the tests of learning ability and the criterion scores (0.08 to 0.66) with substantial overall correlations between the Verbal Learning tests, Analogies and Number Series and all the criterion scores.

Bearing in mind the small size of the English sample and the restriction which must consequently be placed on drawing firm conclusions from the data, it should still be pointed out that the performance of this particular sample lends support to the superior predictive ability of the learning tests in comparison with the measures of intelligence used in this research.

The non-verbal tests of the Wechsler Intelligence Scale show a somewhat poorer but similar predictive validity for the English children, where the correlation coefficients with the criterion scores range from 0.33 to 0.44, than for the Indian children where correlation coefficients range from 0.37 to 0.53 (Table A2.1). The overall predictive validity of a verbal measure of intelligence is evident from the range of correlations between the scores on the WISC Vocabulary sub-test for the English children at the time of the initial testing with the scores on other criterion measures (0·31 to 0·51): this range of values, whilst superior to any one of the non-verbal intelligence tests, is considerably lower than any of the learning ability tests except the Concept Formation test (see Table A2.2) and gives support to the suggestion that tests of learning ability might be a valuable addition to the methods we use to assess the abilities of English children.

3. Comparative data on initial test scores and subsequent attainment

A comparison of the Indian and English children on the initial test scores and the criterion scores was made with a view to discovering any differences in the pattern of their abilities. Differences in the test performance of the Indian boys and the Indian girls was also investigated.

(a) *Comparison of the Indian and English Children on Initial Test Scores and Final Attainment*

The differences between the two samples on the learning ability, intelligence and criterion tests other than the English Picture Vocabulary test are tabulated in Table A2.12. An explanation of the Kolmogorov Smirnov test which was used to assess the significance of the differences between the samples may be found in *Nonparametric Statistics* (Siegel, 1956).

The differences between the two samples on the English Picture Vocabulary Test had to be omitted from this analysis since for the second administration Test 2 was given to the English children in accordance with the norms of the test whereas Test 1 had to be used again for the Indian children. Test 2 is more difficult and would not have been sufficiently discriminating for the Indian children. The two samples could not be compared therefore on this criterion measure.

Marked differences were found in the test performance of the two samples. These are best described by the histograms in Figure 1, which have been determined by scaling the scores of the English children on each test to a mean of 45 and a standard deviation of 15. The English children are represented by a straight line drawn across the chart at level 45. The Indian children are represented by a shaded column having a height equivalent to their mean scaled scores, the scaling constants being based on the English sample.

The differences in the profile of abilities for the two samples can be readily seen in this chart.

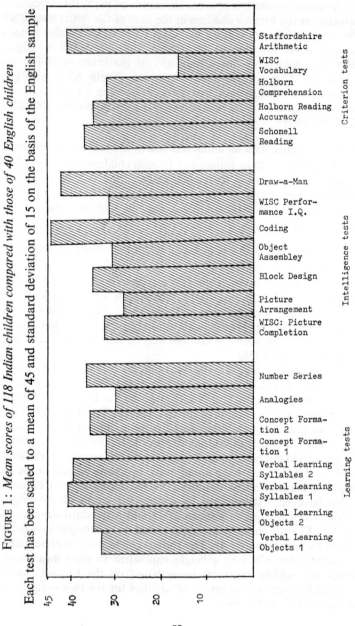

FIGURE 1: *Mean scores of 118 Indian children compared with those of 40 English children*

Each test has been scaled to a mean of 45 and standard deviation of 15 on the basis of the English sample

It is evident from Table A2.10 that the attainment of this sample of English children at the end of their second year in the junior school is significantly in advance of the sample of Indian children, but that the discrepancy is not so great with regard to arithmetic as measured by the Staffordshire test. The English children tend to score significantly higher than the Indian children on the tests of intelligence and learning ability. The learning test where this is not the case, namely Verbal Learning Syllables, correlated highly with all the criterion measures, whereas the two measures of intelligence which do not discriminate between the two samples, namely Draw-a-Man and WISC Coding, have been shown to be relatively poor predictors of educational achievement.

The correlation values for Draw-a-Man and the criterion scores for the Indian children were of the order of $0 \cdot 16$ to $0 \cdot 29$; for the English children the coefficients ranged between $0 \cdot 06$ and $0 \cdot 40$. In the case of WISC Coding, the correlations with the criterion scores ranged between $0 \cdot 11$ and $0 \cdot 22$ for the Indian children and $-0 \cdot 05$ and $0 \cdot 16$ for the English children. It would seem from these data that the learning of nonsense syllables is a relatively culture-fair test for these two cultural groups which, unlike WISC Coding or Draw-a-Man, is related significantly to subsequent learning in school.

The significant differences between the performance of the two samples on all the other tests, however, lends further support to the contention that separate norms should be made available for different cultural groups.

(b) *Sex Differences in the Attainments of Indian Children*

It was thought that differing expectancies on the part of the Indian culture or the host community and differing rates of maturation might be giving rise to differences in the educational attainments of Indian boys and girls. The method used to investigate differences in test performance between Indian and English children was used to investigate any such differences in the initial attainments of the Indian boys and girls of this sample and in their educational achievements at the end of their second year in the junior school. It will be seen from Table A2.11 that no significant differences were found between the sexes at either of the times that their attainments were assessed.

4. Correlations between the teachers' estimates of ability and subsequent attainment

The validity of the teachers' original estimates of the child's ability was examined by correlational analysis for the Indian and English samples. The correlation coefficients are listed in Table 8 from which it is apparent that the teachers' estimates have maintained a high overall predictive validity with the criterion scores in the case of both samples. However, the correlations for the Indian children, although significant, are lower than for the English children and indicate that the teachers predicted less efficiently in the case of the Indian children.

Remembering our earlier discussion of the association between teachers' expectancies and the achievements of their pupils it should be noted here that these estimates are not self-fulfilling prophecies.

The estimates were made by teachers during the child's first term at the junior school and the children were subsequently taught by other teachers. We therefore have evidence of the confidence which may be placed on a teacher's estimate of a child's progress. Nevertheless, it should be remembered that in the case of this sample of immigrant pupils these estimates have been shown to be a second best to the predictive validity of the learning ability tests.

TABLE 8: *Correlation coefficients of teachers' estimates of ability and the criterion scores*

Test	Indian Sample (N=118)	English Sample (N=40)
Schonell Graded Word	0·41	0·64
Holborn Scale Reading Age	0·40	0·74
Holborn Scale Comprehension	0·42	0·73
Staffordshire Arithmetic	0·48	0·44
English Picture Vocabulary	0·39	0·45
WISC Vocabulary	0·37	0·63

CHAPTER FIVE

Concomitant Variations Affecting Educational Progress

INFORMATION concerning the school and the teacher, together with additional pupil variables, was obtained from the teachers and children through interviews and the use of the various questionnaires and rating scales as outlined in Chapter Two. A considerable amount of information was collected and it became possible to analyse statistically the effects on the educational progress of 24 further pupil variables and four main variables to do with the teachers and schools.

Many variables, perhaps important ones, had to be discarded from the correlational analysis owing to their skewed distributions within this particular sample. Thus it was not possible to investigate the effects of remedial teaching in a withdrawal group, for example, since very few children were receiving this. For the same reason it was not possible to investigate the effects of placement in a special class or being taught by an Indian rather than an English teacher using different types of teaching materials and techniques. Factors such as these may well be of paramount importance in the education of our immigrant children, but this research was not designed to investigate the effects of such factors and would have required the study of large samples of children selected according to the particular environmental differences which are being held in question. The variables which did lend themselves to further analysis are listed in Table 9 together with information of the type of statistical analysis carried out. The results of the statistical analyses are to be found in Table A2.12 and Table 12.

1. Discussion of the results

a. *School, Class and Teacher Variables*

i. Proportion of immigrant pupils in the school. The first variable to be examined, namely percentages of immigrant and Indian children in the school, produced a somewhat surprising finding. The sample was divided into two groups: children in group 1 were attending schools with 18 per cent Indians and 32 per cent immigrants or less;

children in group 2 were attending schools where there were more than 18 per cent Indians and 32 per cent immigrant pupils. Children in the schools which had the higher percentages tended to obtain better scores on all the attainment tests (see Table A2.12). The differences between the mean scores of the children in the two groups were not significant, however, and the difference might not have persisted if the percentage of immigrant children increased beyond 59 per cent, which was the maximum in any school in this sample. However, there is a definite trend and there are several factors with which this might be associated.

TABLE 9: *List of school, teacher, class and pupil variables with reference to the statistical analysis to be carried out*

A. *t- or F-tests of significance between mean scores on the six criterion tests for children categorized on:*
   1. Percentage of Indians and Immigrants in School
   2. Teacher's Attitude towards Indian Children
   3. Frequency of Testing Reading, Arithmetic and Spelling
   4. Experience of Teacher

B. *Principal components analysis of the six criterion tests and the following 24 pupil variables:*
   1. Help with School Work at Home
   2. Parent's Attitude to Homework
   3. Child's Attitude to Homework
   4. Attendance at Temple
   5. Father's Dress
   6. Language with Father
   7. Language with Mother
   8. Language with Friends
   9. Total Language Score
   10. Test Behaviour Rating 1: Confidence
   11. Test Behaviour Rating 2: Concentration
   12. Test Behaviour Rating 3: Co-operation
   13. Mother and Work
   14. Best Friends
   15. Length of Infant Schooling
   16. Number of Teachers in Junior School
   17. Attendance at School
   18. Integration Rating
   19. Attitude to Work Rating
   20. Pupil's School Questionnaire Attitude A: Attitude to School
   21. Pupil's School Questionnaire Attitude B: Relationship with Teacher
   22. Pupil's School Questionnaire Attitude E: Social Adjustment
   23. Pupil's School Questionnaire Attitude F: Anxiety
   24. Pupil's School Questionnaire Attitude G: Importance of Doing Well

ii. Teacher attitude towards immigrant pupils. A possible explanation might be found in differences in teacher attitude, more favourably disposed teachers being found in the schools where there are larger numbers of immigrants. There is an association between higher total scores on the teachers' attitude scale and achievement of the Indian pupils on the English Picture Vocabulary Test (Table A2.12) only, and further analysis of the data revealed that as suspected the teachers in the group of schools with higher percentages of immigrants showed significantly more favourable opinions about Indian children on all three factors of the attitude scale (Table 10).

TABLE 10: *t-tests between means for teacher attitude factors by school group*

Group 1 = Teachers in schools with 18% Indian and 32% immigrant pupils or less.
Group 2 = Teachers in schools with more than 18% Indians and 32% immigrant pupils.

Factor	Group 1	Group 2	t-Value
A. Attitude towards Indian child as a pupil	51·89	59·15	5·55***
B. Attitude towards having Indian children in the class	52·00	60·02	5·74***
C. Attitude towards intellectual capacity of an Indian child	38·11	42·94	5·04***

(*** significant at the 0·1% level)

The significant association between the school groups and the children's progress might have been caused by actual differences in the abilities of the children rather than by the teacher attitude. In order to investigate this possibility t-tests were carried out on the differences between the means of the children according to school group on their learning test scores. These are given in Table 11.

None of these t-values is significant, which indicates that the differences in both teacher attitude and subsequent pupil achievement between the two school groups is not dependent on any difference in the distribution of ability between the two school groups.

Robinson (1950) has drawn attention to the important consideration that correlations obtained when the school is used as the statistical unit cannot be assumed to be equivalent to correlations

TABLE 11: *t-tests between means on the learning test scores by school group*

Group 1 = Pupils attending schools with 18% Indian and 32% immigrant pupils or less.
Group 2 = Pupils attending schools with more than 18% Indian and 32% immigrant pupils.

Learning Test	MEANS Group 1	Group 2	t-Values
Verbal Learning Objects: Score 1	16·89	18·37	0·65
Verbal Learning Objects: Score 2	5·13	5·69	0·89
Verbal Learning Syllables: Score 1	13·01	14·93	1·04
Verbal Learning Syllables: Score 2	5·25	5·80	0·83
Analogies	4·09	3·97	0·24
Concept Formation: Score 1	11·86	10·72	0·81
Concept Formation: Score 2	5·08	5·28	0·65
Number Series	8·07	8·85	−1·20

obtained when the individual is used as the unit, and this must also be borne in mind in attempting to interpret the association between the attitudes of groups of teachers and pupil progress.

When the teachers' attitude (total score) was correlated with the criterion scores using the teacher, rather than groups of teachers, as the statistical unit a small positive trend was found (Table 12).

TABLE 12: *Correlations between teachers' attitude score and criterion scores*

Group 1 = Schools with 18% Indian and 32% immigrant pupils or less.
Group 2 = Schools with more than 18% Indian and 32% immigrant pupils.

	TOTAL SAMPLE Teacher N=35 Pupil N=109	SCHOOL GROUP 1 Teacher N=23 Pupil N=62	SCHOOL GROUP 2 Teacher N=12 Pupil N=47
Schonell Reading Test	0·13	0·28*	−0·07
Holborn Scale Reading Accuracy	0·15	0·19	0·06
Holborn Scale Comprehension	0·12	0·17	−0·08
Staffordshire Arithmetic	0·06	0·07	−0·06
English Picture Vocabulary	0·16	0·07	−0·02
WISC Vocabulary	0·15	0·12	−0·07

(*significant at the 5% level)

The correlations were also calculated within the two school groups separately (Table 12). In the case of the Group 1 schools, (those with lower percentages of immigrants), the trend remains the same and reaches the five per cent level of significance with the Schonell Reading Test. Group 2 schools, which contain the more favourably disposed teachers, reveal small negative correlations, except for the Holborn Scale Reading Age where there is a small positive association. The difference in trends between the two school groups would lead one to consider that the effect of an unfavourable attitude has a more depressing effect on the children's achievements than a favourable attitude has in aiding their achievements.

In order to make a more precise analysis of the relationship between teacher attitude and the actual ability of the Indian children in their class, the correlation was calculated between the general estimate of ability by the class teachers summed over two years and the teacher attitude score of the class teacher in year two. A coefficient of 0·27 was obtained which is significant at the one per cent level, indicating an association between the two variables.

The relationship between the teacher attitude and the actual ability of their pupils was endorsed by correlations calculated between the total score on the teachers' attitude scale and educational achievement, partialling out the factor of the teacher's ratings of ability. Table 13 lists these partial correlations. The coefficients were all very small and smaller than the correlations between the total teacher attitude score and educational achievements when ability was not held constant (see Table 12 and Table A2.12).

TABLE 13: *Correlations between teacher attitudes and criterion scores partialling out ratings of ability*

	General Ability Rating over 2 Years
1. Schonell Reading	−0·03
2. Holborn Reading Accuracy	−0·01
3. Holborn Comprehension	−0·05
4. Staffordshire Arithmetic	−0·16
5. English Picture Vocabulary	−0·02
6. WISC Vocabulary	0·00

This suggests that when the effect of the child's own ability as rated by the teacher is removed the relationship between teacher attitude and attainment is more tenuous and makes it imperative to interpret the association between the attitude of groups of teachers and educational achievement with caution.

It is still not possible to sort out the relationship between the teacher attitude and the pupil's achievements in the Group 1 versus Group 2 schools. The association may be due to the presence of other factors such as the Indian children finding it easier to settle into schools where there are more Indian children or those schools which have higher percentages of immigrants might well be devoting more time and effort to the teaching of basic arithmetic and reading skills. The presence of more favourably disposed teachers in such schools may or may not be crucial. This question certainly merits further investigation but unfortunately it cannot be pursued with these data owing to the small number of teachers and schools involved.

iii. Frequency of attainment testing. Referring back to Table A2.12, it will be seen that there were only two further significant relationships between teacher or class variables and educational achievement. These are to do with frequency of testing.

The frequency with which the children were tested for reading over the two-year period shows a trend for better results on the attainment tests, other than arithmetic, for the group which had been tested more often. None of these t-values reached significance and when the effects of testing reading in year 2 only were examined the same trend is not confirmed and is in fact, reversed with a significant inverse relationship between frequency of testing and attainment on the English Picture Vocabulary Test. Possibly, teachers who continue in a test-bound approach to their pupils' progress are inhibiting the development of a wider vocabulary and other skills.

This suggestion is supported from the tendency for the children who were tested least often in arithmetic and in spelling in year 2 to do better in all their attainments. This relationship reaches the five per cent level of significance in the case of the inverse relationship between the frequency of testing spelling and reading accuracy as measured by the Holborn Scale.

This trend is supported by the effects of frequency of testing on achievement in arithmetic. Frequent testing followed by less frequent testing again seems to give better results than the reverse order of testing frequency.

iv. Teachers' experience. Looking at the last section of Table A2.12, it will be seen that teachers with more years teaching ex-perience in year 2 tend to get poorer results with reading and vocabulary. It seems that whilst there is a trend for better progress to be associated with having more experienced teachers in the first year this relationship tends to be reversed and sometimes significantly so if continued through the second year.

It is possible that the experienced teachers are also the frequent testers and that the children benefit from a more formal test orientated approach in their first year followed by a less formal and freer atmosphere in their second year, but it was not possible to examine the combined effect of these two variables in the course of this research owing to the small number of teachers.

b. *Pupil Variables*

Product moment correlations had already been computed between the 24 variables listed in Table 9 and the six criterion scores (Table A2·1). A principal components analysis was carried out on these variables and ten factors were extracted accounting for 68·5 per cent of the variance. An oblique rotated solution was then computed by the Promax procedure (see Appendix Three). The factor loadings are given in Table 14. Factors 3, 7 and 8 have been omitted from the table since there were no significant loadings on any of the criterion tests. Owing to computer costs five of the pupil variables retained for analysis had to be rejected from the principal components analysis. It was decided to drop five of the attitude scale scores from the Pupil's School Questionnaire, retaining those which were felt likely from the point of view of the Indian children to be most significant for their educational progress. All ten attitudes scales were used in a subse-quent comparative analysis of these Indian children with a larger sample of English children, the results of which are described in the last section of the present chapter.

The first factor extracted in the principal components analysis links the criterion measures with the teachers' ratings on the child's integration with English children, the child's attitude to work, the child's own attitude to school and feelings about doing well. (Attitudes A and G of the Pupil's School Questionnaire.) The criterion scores are also linked to the child's ability to concentrate and willingness to co-operate, as rated by the psychologist, during the learning tests, and to the amount of English they are able to speak with their mothers.

Factor 2 can be identified as a language factor which has no close connection with the criterion scores other than vocabulary but is linked to ratings of the child's confidence and ability to integrate. Thus it would seem that the children who talk more English at home and who are spoken to more often in English are not necessarily doing better academically in school but the extent to which they use English may well help them personally and socially.

Factor 4 indicates an association between school achievements, particularly in arithmetic, and the child's concentration and co-operation as rated by the psychologist, also with the child's attitude to work as rated by his teachers and the importance the child himself

TABLE 14: *Oblique primary factor loadings of 24 pupil variables and six criterion scores*

(Factors 3, 7 and 8 have been omitted from this table since there were no significant loadings on the criterion tests. Factor loadings of 0·25 and less have also been omitted.)

VARIABLE	1	2	4	5
Schonell Reading Test	0·89		0·33	0·27
Holborn Scale Reading Age	0·91		0·29	
Holborn Scale Comprehension	0·93		0·33	0·26
Staffordshire Arithmetic	0·62		0·58	
English Picture Vocabulary	0·80	0·28	0·33	0·35
WISC Vocabulary	0·83	0·38	0·36	0·37
Help with School Work				0·61
Parents' Attitude to Homework				
Child's Attitude to Homework				
Attendance at Temple		0·30	−0·32	
Father's Dress			−0·53	0·31
Language with Father		0·79		
Language with Mother	0·35	0·78		
Language with Friends		0·53		−0·39
Total Language Score		0·87		
Test Behaviour Rating 1		0·40	0·45	
Test Behaviour Rating 2	0·42		0·70	0·26
Test Behaviour Rating 3	0·41		0·70	0·27
Mother and Work				
Best Friends				
Length of Infant Schooling		0·30		
Number of Teachers				
Attendance at School	0·28		0·28	0·54
Integration Rating	0·59	0·41		
Attitude to Work Rating	0·54		0·52	0·30
Attitude A Attitude to School	0·41			0·51
Attitude B Attitude to Teacher				
Attitude E Social Adjustment				
Attitude F Anxiety				
Attitude G Importance of Doing Well	0·40		0·41	

TABLE 14—*continued*

VARIABLE	6	9	10
Schonell Reading Test		0·40	
Holborn Scale Reading Age		0·43	
Holborn Scale Comprehension		0·43	
Staffordshire Arithmetic	0·45	0·42	0·58
English Picture Vocabulary		0·34	
WISC Vocabulary		0·47	
Help with School Work			
Parents' Attitude to Homework			
Child's Attitude to Homework			
Attendance at Temple		0·29	
Father's Dress			
Language with Father			
Language with Mother			
Language with Friends			−0·26
Total Language Score			
Test Behaviour Rating 1		0·39	0·33
Test Behaviour Rating 2		0·26	
Test Behaviour Rating 3		0·35	
Mother and Work			0·64
Best Friends	0·54		
Length of Infant Schooling	−0·29		−0·65
Number of Teachers			
Attendance at School	0·38		
Integration Rating		0·46	
Attitude to Work Rating	0·33	0·49	0·47
Attitude A Attitude to School		0·69	
Attitude B Attitude to Teacher		0·62	
Attitude E Social Adjustment	0·74		
Attitude F Anxiety			
Attitude G Importance of Doing Well		0·70	0·44

attaches to doing well (Attitude G). This factor also points to a negative association between progress at school and the father's style of dressing and the regularity of the family's attendance at temple, both of which might be considered as signs of perpetuating an allegiance to the Indian culture.

Factor 5 has positive loadings on the criterion scores and links together the amount of help the child actually receives with his school work at home and his attitude to school and attendance at school. This factor might be identified as a kind of conscientiousness which is being actively supported with help at home.

Factor 6 links a tendency to do well in arithmetic with poor scores on the social adjustment attitude scale (Attitude E of the Pupil's

School Questionnaire) and the tendency to choose only Indian children as friends.

Factor 9 shows a tendency for children who score well on the confidence and co-operation ratings to make progress in school and to have favourable attitudes to school and their teacher and to attach importance to doing well.

Factor 10 brings out the relative lack of importance of the length of infant schooling in explaining variance on the criterion measures. This confirms the low correlations between these variables (Table A2.1). This factor also brings out a small positive link between mothers going out to work and the child's progress in arithmetic.

The associations between these pupil variables and progress in school are best summarized by now looking at Table 15 which gives

TABLE 15: *Correlations between the oblique primary factors of the* 24 *pupil variables and six criterion scores*†

FACTOR	1	2	4	5	6	9	10
1	1·00						
2	−0·32	1·00					
4	−0·38	0·00	1·00				
5	−0·36	−0·02	0·14	1·00			
6	0·17	0·09	−0·28	−0·17	1·00		
9	−0·53	0·27	−0·26	0·26	−0·07	1·00	
10	0·23	0·07	−0·48	−0·08	0·19	−0·26	1·00

(†Factors 3, 7 and 8 have been omitted from this table since there were no significant loadings on the criterion tests.)

the correlations between the ten oblique factors having loadings on the criterion measures. By re-ordering the correlation coefficients it will be seen that:

1. the criterion scores are positively correlated with the child's attitudes to school, to the teacher and to the importance of doing well; also associated are the child's confidence and co-operation as rated by the psychologist (Factors 1 and 9);

2. the associations between Factors 1 and 4 link achievement in school with the child's attitude to work, with his confidence and co-operation and an absence of both his father's continued wish to wear the Indian style of clothes and the family's regular attendance at the Sikh temple;

3. the correlations between Factors 1 and 5 bring out the relationship between conscientiousness and active help with school work at home with progress at school;

4. factors 1 and 2 correlate sufficiently to signify an association between the criterion scores and the effects of speaking more English at home, the child's confidence and his ability to integrate at school.

c. *Comparison of the Attitudes to School of Indian and English Children*

The data obtained from the Pupil's School Questionnaire with the Indian children was compared with the data from a sample of one thousand nine-year-old English children obtained in the NFER Streaming Research project (Barker Lunn, 1970). The differences in the distributions of their scores are set out in Table 16.[1]

TABLE 16: *Comparative distribution of scores of Indian children and nine-year-old English children on ten pupil attitudes*

ATTITUDE	LEVEL OF SIGNIFICANCE	DETAILS
A Attitude to School	0·1%	Indians > English
B Relationship with Teacher	1·0%	Indians > English
C Academic Self Image	NS	
D Attitude to Class	1·0%	Indians < English
E Social Adjustment	0·1%	Indians < English
F Anxiety	NS	
G Importance of doing well	NS	
H Conforming versus non-conforming	NS	
I Other Image of Class	5%	Indians > English
J Interest in School Work	NS	

From this table it will be seen that the Indian children have a significantly more favourable attitude towards school and their class teachers, but are significantly less well adjusted socially (as measured by Attitude Scale E) and score significantly worse on items which have to do with how well they are getting on with other children in their class (Scale D). The wider implications of these findings will be discussed in the concluding chapter.

[1] Kolmogorov-Smirnov tests were used to investigate the differences in the distributions of the scores in the same way as the different samples had been investigated on the learning ability tests (see Siegel, 1956).

CHAPTER SIX

Conclusions

1. Summary of findings

(a) *The Tests of Learning Ability*

The principal aim of this study was to devise a new type of test which could be used to assess the learning abilities of children with all degrees of linguistic and other cultural handicaps. The major part of the research was therefore concerned with the development of a battery of learning tests and these were individually administered and standardized on samples of seven- to eight-year-old Indian and English children. The tasks involved in doing the tests were devised in such a way as to enlist a variety of mental skills of a kind which were thought necessary for making progress with learning at school.

In Chapter Three the test-retest reliabilities of the different methods of scoring the tests were discussed and on the basis of these, five out of the six experimental learning tests were retained for the validation analysis. For three of the tests, Verbal Learning Objects, Verbal Learning Syllables and Concept Formation, two methods of scoring were retained and for two tests, Analogies and Number Series, only one scoring method each was retained. The memory test was rejected from further analysis since it was found to be unreliable.

The unreliability of the memory test was not surprising considering the small sample of behaviour on which the score is based. It is possible that a similar test could well be a valuable addition to the battery if it were adapted into more of a learning task in which the child could be given several trials at remembering a larger collection of items, much as in the procedure outlined by Ord (1967) where articles of different size, shape, colour and texture are observed and subsequently to be distinguished from objects added whilst the child looks elsewhere.

A factor analysis was carried out on the selected scoring methods which indicated that there are three underlying components in the learning test battery. This was confirmed by a principal components

72

analysis of the learning ability, intelligence and criterion test scores where a verbal factor and a non-verbal factor was identified within the learning test battery as well as a less marked division within the non-verbal learning tests; the Analogies and Number Series showing a closer relationship with each other than with the Concept Formation test.

Despite this grouping of tests within the battery it was considered premature to attempt any method of combining the subtest scores. It was felt that such a step could be more appropriately taken if, after further development of the tests, similar clusterings were found with different age groups.

The children had also been assessed on the Performance Scale of the Wechsler Intelligence Scale for Children and on the Goodenough Draw-a-Man Test. This made it possible to estimate the relative validity of the learning tests and the non-verbal intelligence tests in predicting achievement in school. There was no evidence either from the original correlations or from the factor analysis of any close overlap between intelligence and learning tests, and this was further confirmed by the regression analysis.

The regression analysis was carried out in order to examine more fully the relative predictive powers of the two types of test and the teacher's original estimate of the child's ability, an assessment which had been made after the child had been in the teacher's class for the best part of his first term in the junior school. The regression analysis highlighted the validity of the verbal learning tests in predicting subsequent school achievement. Although the teacher's estimate of ability did correlate significantly with the criterion scores it was only selected in the regression analysis in connection with the Staffordshire Arithmetic test, but even here one of the learning tests, Number Series, was shown to explain more of the variance in the arithmetic scores. Of the intelligence tests, the WISC Picture Arrangement adds significantly to the Verbal Learning Tests in predicting progress in reading accuracy and comprehension and the WISC Performance Scale IQ is selected as a significant predictor of level of vocabulary as measured by the English Picture Vocabulary Tests, but again one of the learning tests, Verbal Learning Objects, has a clear superiority as regards predictive validity.

The two Verbal Learning tests and the Number Series test explained most of the variance in the criterion and evidence was provided by a further regression analysis that one of the verbal learning tests, Verbal Learning of Objects, and the Number Series test are a valid short method of predicting the criteria. From the first regression analysis the Verbal Learning of Objects and the Verbal Learning of Syllables appear to overlap in function and they also have high intercorrelations.

Further examination of the behaviour of these two tests when the scores of the two samples, Indian and English, were compared, suggests that the Verbal Learning of Syllables is the less culturally biased of the two tests; it is also highly reliable with a test-retest coefficient of 0·77 and would be a relatively straightforward type of test to develop and administer with different age and cultural groups. There are strong grounds, therefore, for retaining this test within the battery and in view of Jensen's research on different types of learning there are also grounds for retaining the type of paired associate learning involved in the Verbal Learning of Objects. The work of Otto (1961) which shows that paired associate learning has relevance to school learning, namely reading ability, independently of IQ is also of interest here.

Jensen (1967b, 1968) in reporting a series of experiments makes the suggestion that the culturally retarded child will learn a serial list more efficiently than a paired-associate list. This has been borne out by the present study in which the paired associate learning, Verbal Learning Objects, shows a significant difference between the two cultural groups not present in the case of serial learning, Verbal Learning Syllables. Jensen has found that paired-associate learning is greatly facilitated by some form of verbal mediational process (Jensen and Rohwer 1963) whereas serial learning is not significantly influenced.

On the basis of this and further research (Jensen and Rohwer 1965) in which it was found that ability in paired associate learning increases with age up to eighteen years, presumably on account of an increasing use of verbal facilitative devices, while there appears to be no similar increase in the ability to learn a serial list beyond age eight, Jensen proposes that serial learning more nearly measures learning ability relatively unaffected by the person's previous verbal experiences. In his earlier study of retarded, average and gifted children (Jensen 1963), he concluded that many children viewed as retarded have merely failed to learn the verbal mediators which facilitate school learning. He found that a sample of children who had been classified as retarded educationally and were in special remedial classes produced a significant improvement in a learning test when they were required to verbalize while learning. The research of Moely *et al.* (1969) in which simple instructions are shown to overcome initial weakness on tasks involving recall of objects which can be conceptually clustered lends further hopes to remedial intervention in cases where basic learning ability has not been fully realized. Jensen suggests that without the habit of verbalizing either overtly or covertly 'even a child with a perfectly normal nervous system in the terms of fundamental learning ability will appear to be retarded and indeed is retarded so long as he does not use verbal mediators in learning'. Jensen considers that the discrepancy between the scores on the two types of learning task should be indicative of the degree of verbal underdevelopment in relation to the child's basic learning equipment. He has not yet made any large-scale investigation of this as a function of cultural group or social class, although we do have his study of Mexican-American and Anglo-American children (1961) where the Mexican-American children revealed superior serial learning ability, but inferior paired associate learning ability, compared to the Anglo-American children of the same IQ. A great deal more needs to be known about cultural differences in these two forms of learning before they can be used as diagnostic tools.

An examination of the progress of the children whose initial scores on the Holborn Reading Scale were zero in relation to their scores on the learning tests lends further support for the merits of the Verbal Learning Syllables test, but a combination of the learning tests and the teacher's estimate and intelligence test scores in the ways indicated by the first regression analysis would yield a richer and more valid instrument of prediction.

The performance of the English children lends support to the relatively superior predictive ability of the learning tests in comparison with the measures of intelligence used in this research. In fact, the non-verbal tests of intelligence showed greater predictive validity for the Indian children than for the English children, possibly because an additional task was involved as far as the Indian children were concerned in understanding what they had to do and in adapting to a new situation.

(b) *Differences in Test Performance of Indian and English Children*

Significant differences were found in favour of the English children with regard to their achievements as measured by the criterion tests and marked differences were found in the initial test scores on the learning and intelligence tests between the two samples. No sex differences in attainment were found within the Indian sample.

As already mentioned, the Verbal Learning of Syllables is a

relatively culture-fair test for these two groups, which unlike WISC Coding or the Draw-a-Man Test is related significantly to subsequent learning in school. The wide difference in the performance of the two groups on the other tests, however, gives further evidence for the need to make separate norms available for different cultural groups.

(c) *The Variables Affecting Educational Progress*

It will be recalled that an investigation of many of the variables which were thought likely to be affecting the educational progress of the Indian children had to be discarded from the main analyses owing to some very uneven distributions of the variables within this relatively small sample.

Of the school, class and teacher variables which did lend themselves to statistical analysis, an association was found between teacher attitudes, the proportion of immigrants in the school and the children's achievements at the end of the second year in the junior school. The complexities of this association were fully discussed in the previous chapter. Briefly, it was thought that the fact that Indian children made better progress in schools where there were larger numbers of immigrants might have been because the presence of a larger number of their compatriots enabled these young children to adjust more quickly to their surroundings or because more time and effort was spent in teaching the basic reading and number skills in such schools. On the other hand their progress may have been more to do with being taught by teachers with a more positive attitude to Indian children since there was a tendency for teacher attitude and achievements to be associated and there was a significant difference in teacher attitude between the schools with larger or smaller proportions of immigrant pupils. It was not possible to reach any conclusions with the present data and further research is clearly necessary.

A trend was also found between achievement, being taught by more experienced teachers and frequent testing of attainments in the first year. But this appeared to act only as an auspicious initiation process which if continued throughout the second year became associated with lower scores on the attainment tests.

It was also necessary to discard many of the pupil variables from the statistical analysis—amongst these being the teacher ratings on the child's emotional adjustment. Although the unreliability of the scales precluded any further investigation, it must also be pointed out that the distributions of the ratings which were made by the class teachers at the end of year 1 and year 2 were on both occasions very skewed. As a group the children were rated highly for adjustment and the scale which was constructed specially for this research proved undiscriminating.

Vernon (1940) in his book *The Measurement of Abilities* claims that the rating technique is the best single method for assessing psychological qualities although different raters differ widely in assessing the same person. For this research perhaps the precaution should have been taken of obtaining the average rating for the various aspects of emotional adjustment given by several observers. But the scales may still have proved undiscriminating since teachers frequently expressed the opinion that Indian children tend to be emotionally more stable than the children of other cultural groups, including English children. This is an impression which the present investigation would seem to support and it may well have something to do with what appears to be relatively settled and secure home life amongst Indian peoples. Emotional maladjustment may not be a very important variable in this sample, and excluding it from further analysis may not have caused much information to be lost.

The principal components analysis of the 24 pupil variables which were retained for analysis and the six criterion scores extracted ten factors. The variables showed slight associations with the criterion scores in the expected direction, e.g. attitude to school, ability to integrate and ratings on confidence, concentration and co-operation, but the amount of English spoken at home was not associated with the criterion scores as highly as might be expected, neither was the effect of length of infant schooling in England.

Although attendance at school clearly helps mental development in general, there is very little evidence for or against any particular kind of schooling in favouring educational progress, particularly of the kind of progress which is being assessed in this study which is rather a restricted type of assessment and does not include any assessment of general knowledge and other skills which the children may have been developing. All except two of the Indian children had earlier been attending school either in this country or abroad and there is no evidence that one type of schooling had been more favourable than another in preparing the children for the junior school. On the other hand it must be remembered that all except fourteen had attended infant school for two terms or more, so perhaps this is a crucial factor which is being concealed by the small size of the sample and which it is not possible to investigate further with the present data.

In summarizing the trends within these particular pupils and their environment which are conducive to educational progress it would seem that the attitudes of the teachers and the pupils are more important than any other factor. In comparison with English children of similar age it was found that the attitudes of the Indian children towards school and teachers are considerably more favourable than in the case of their English counterparts. This is an auspicious finding and one which emphasizes the responsibility of the teachers to sponsor this positive attitude. The possibility that the Indian children themselves may not be experiencing sufficient augmentation of these feelings is indicated by their significantly poorer scores on social adjustment and their attitude to class scale (see Table 16).

2. Implications of the findings and suggestions for future research

The main indication for future research arising out of the findings of this study concerns the further development of the learning tests themselves. Clearly they could add to the diagnostic validity of the range of tests already available to psychologists in assessing the abilities of immigrant children and perhaps they would also be a valuable addition to the methods used to assess English children.

Individual tests of ability are needed to diagnose the reasons for retardation and backwardness in school and in this connection are required as a basis for making decisions such as a referral for remedial teaching, for psychotherapy or for placement in a special class or school. There is also the problem of assessing the abilities of immigrant children when they are transferring to the secondary stage of their education. Many of these children are unable to master English sufficiently to be selected to profit from such an education. Tests of learning ability might well add to the recommendations we make for immigrant children at this important stage in their school careers. In this connection, in areas where secondary selection systems continue, Local Education Authorities could also be doing a service to follow up the subsequent performance of immigrant children relative to their test scores at eleven-plus so that we can begin to have some data on the predictive validity of the tests on the basis of which the recommendations are currently being made.

Attention has also been drawn recently to the need for the development of methods of assessing the potential of coloured school leavers before entering employment and is one of the recommendations for research made by the House of Commons Select Committee on Race Relations and Immigration (1969).

We have seen in the course of this research that a teacher's judgements about an Indian child's ability tend to be less valid as predictors of achievement than his assessment of English children and there is no doubt that testing could be of great value in defining the abilities and disabilities in our immigrant pupils. But these tests of learning ability like every other individual psychological test require to be administered by trained testers. The danger of taking test results at their face value was strongly emphasized in Chapter One and tests which could be used as a basis for making long-term and major decisions must be used responsibly and with caution by suitably qualified administrators.

It may be possible to develop similar kinds of learning tests which could be administered by teachers in a group form but in the words of the Report of the Brent Teacher's Association (1969) it would seem 'much more profitable for teachers to observe the child's progress in a sympathetic and understanding school environment and to employ special materials and methods of teaching rather than to predict or judge through tests'.

The danger of relying too much on tests cannot be too strongly emphasized. No matter how wide a battery of tests we use, we cannot depend solely on the tests themselves in taking decisions about a particular child any more than we can expect to decrease the proportion of culturally disadvantaged or verbally underdeveloped children simply by diagnosing their condition. We also depend on the use, and the intelligent use, of tests by our psychologists and upon the competence and interest of all concerned in seeking and carrying out their recommendations.

Secondly there is clearly a pressing need for research in the whole area of teacher-pupil attitudes but particularly so in the field of race relations. A research project was set up in April 1970 at the NFER which has as part of its brief an investigation into the relationships between immigrant pupils, their classmates and their teachers and it is to be hoped that this and other investigations will help to mobilize a receptive and sponsoring attitude towards the individuality of all these children in our schools.

In conclusion it should be mentioned that in talking with the teachers involved in this research, it was clear that not only did they feel a need for tests and new teaching materials, they also felt that these immigrant children needed more individual attention. The teachers would welcome the use of non-teaching staff within the school to help them in providing the opportunity for more individual conversation. They felt this would be preferable to the establishment of special classes or centres.

Some of the teachers also felt the need to extend the school's influence into non-school time through organizing sports, hobby groups and particularly in organizing different kinds of outings for the children which would enlarge their experience of their new surroundings.

It was also thought that the adjustment of the immigrant children to the new expectancies of school would be enhanced by promoting greater understanding of the educational process amongst their parents. A recommendation for closer contact between home and school has been made in a recent report concerning the problems of coloured school leavers by the House of Commons Select Committee on Race Relations and Immigration (1969). This report not only outlines the conflicts and problems which immigrant children may encounter at school but it gives specific directions for maintaining closer relations with the parents. The aims and methods of the school could be explained through more direct means of communication than the usual Parent-Teacher Association meetings and it was felt by many of the teachers interviewed that smaller informal meetings at school together with the opportunity for home visiting would be a more appropriate way of interpreting the school's programme to the immigrant families.

The final responsibility, however, rests with all of us not only to keep in mind the insidious effects of social isolation on psychological development but to act accordingly and thereby promote the fulfilment of the abilities of all the disadvantaged children in our schools.

APPENDIX ONE

The Teachers' Attitude Scale

THIS scale attempts to assess three aspects of a teacher's attitude towards Indian pupils. The attitude areas were defined as a result of exploratory research with samples of teachers teaching in schools where ten percent or more of the pupils were Indian, excluding schools from which the Indian children for this research had been selected.

Statements collected during the course of interviews with 25 primary and secondary school teachers concerning their opinions about Indian children were assembled into a preliminary questionnaire. This questionnaire was given to another sample of primary school teachers all of whom were having the experience of teaching at least four Indian children in one class. The teachers were asked to indicate their degree of agreement or disagreement with each statement and their responses were subjected to a principal components analysis. Three distinct factors were extracted and the final version of the questionnaire was constructed on the basis of the factor loadings, reliabilities and frequency distributions of the individual statements.

Table A1.1 gives the reliability coefficients for each of the factor scales as determined by Cronbach's alpha-coefficient (Cronbach, L. J., 1951) and the names of the three attitude areas.

TABLE A1.1: *Reliabilities of factor scales for teachers' attitudes*

	TITLE	RELIABILITY COEFFICIENT
Scale A	Attitude towards Indian child as a pupil	0·91
Scale B	Attitude towards having Indian children in the class	0·89
Scale C	Attitude towards intellectual capacity of an Indian child	0·82

The statements incorporated in the final version of the scales were the following:

1. Indian children are an interesting addition to a class.

2. Indian children seriously hinder the progress of the class.

3. You get slow learners among the English children just as often as among the Indians.

4. The Indian children work only when they are told to.

5. English children like having some Indians in the class.

6. Even when the Indian children can speak fluent English, I still find them difficult to get on with.

7. The Indians are often the less intelligent children.

8. Indian children are pleasant to have in the class.

9. Indian children cannot be bothered to work hard.

10. Indian children are not backward because of lack of ability.

11. I would not welcome more than six Indian children in my class.

12. Indian children take their work very seriously.

13. I think English children really do have more ability to learn than Indian children.

14. Most of the Indian children are working as hard as they can.

15. I do not think we should concern ourselves with the cultural backgrounds of the Indian children.

16. Indian children have good powers of concentration.

17. Indian children give up as soon as things start to get difficult.

18. Indian children are just as intelligent as our children.

19. Indian children could not care less about their work.

20. I think it is up to us to help Indian children mix in as much as possible.

21. You have to work very hard to get Indian children to think for themselves.

22. There are very few lazy Indian children.

23. I cannot blame English children for not wanting to play with Indian children.

24. Indian children are always ready to settle down and do some work.

25. English children work more methodically than Indian children.

26. I really enjoy teaching Indian children.

27. Unless you push them, Indian children will not work.

APPENDIX TWO

Statistical Tables

TABLE A2.1: *Correlation matrix of 53 pupil variables 1: Indian sample*

		1	2	3	4	5	6
WISC Picture Completion	1	1·00					
WISC Picture Arrangement	2	0·33	1·00				
WISC Block Design	3	0·26	0·22	1·00			
WISC Object Assembly	4	0·27	0·37	0·33	1·00		
WISC Coding	5	0·20	0·17	0·07	0·22	1·00	
WISC Performance Scale I.Q.	6	0·66	0·54	0·58	0·64	0·59	1·00
Analogies	7	0·36	0·31	0·45	0·27	0·04	0·40
Verbal Learning Objects 1	8	0·38	0·24	0·14	0·12	0·13	0·32
Verbal Learning Objects 2	9	0·35	0·25	0·17	0·08	0·10	0·29
Verbal Learning Syllables 1	10	0·36	0·18	0·17	0·16	0·14	0·34
Verbal Learning Syllables 2	11	0·37	0·21	0·17	0·13	0·25	0·39
Concept Formation 1	12	0·35	0·22	0·27	0·16	−0·02	0·29
Concept Formation 2	13	0·39	0·21	0·28	0·12	0·09	0·34
Number Series	14	0·37	0·31	0·54	0·43	0·13	0·53
Draw-A-Man	15	0·33	0·20	0·27	0·23	0·03	0·34
Date of Testing	16	−0·06	0·05	0·14	0·14	−0·05	0·00
Date of Birth	17	−0·14	0·00	−0·20	−0·07	0·46	0·07
Sex	18	−0·02	−0·01	−0·02	−0·24	0·02	−0·06
Schonell Reading Age	19	0·40	0·36	0·13	0·17	0·17	0·37
Holborn Scale: Reading Age	20	0·40	0·39	0·15	0·15	0·21	0·40
Holborn Scale: Comprehension	21	0·47	0·37	0·22	0·24	0·18	0·45
Staffordshire Arithmetic	22	0·39	0·26	0·34	0·37	0·11	0·43
English Picture Vocabulary	23	0·51	0·45	0·23	0·39	0·22	0·53
WISC Vocabulary	24	0·56	0·43	0·21	0·33	0·15	0·49
Teacher's Estimate of Ability	25	0·27	0·26	0·34	0·22	0·13	0·38
Help with School Work	26	0·02	0·20	0·06	0·00	−0·06	0·04
Parents' Attitude to Homework	27	0·06	−0·04	−0·08	−0·05	0·03	−0·04
Child's Attitude to Homework	28	0·16	−0·04	−0·03	−0·14	0·08	0·01
Attendance at Temple	29	−0·10	0·04	−0·02	−0·14	−0·03	−0·10
Father's Dress	30	0·08	0·07	0·00	0·16	0·17	0·15
Language with Father	31	0·04	0·07	−0·12	−0·21	0·06	−0·05
Language with Mother	32	0·12	0·24	0·09	0·03	0·10	0·16
Language with Friends	33	0·01	0·00	−0·19	−0·15	−0·02	−0·12
Total Language Score	34	0·11	0·10	−0·04	−0·08	−0·01	0·02
Test Behaviour Rating 1	35	0·06	0·02	−0·03	0·03	0·05	0·05
Test Behaviour Rating 2	36	0·38	0·16	0·29	0·24	0·18	0·41
Test Behaviour Rating 3	37	0·33	0·14	0·17	0·12	0·22	0·36
Mother and Work	38	0·16	0·04	0·13	−0·03	0·00	0·09
Best Friends	39	−0·06	0·20	0·02	0·30	−0·12	0·06
Length of Infant Schooling	40	0·11	0·20	−0·06	0·15	0·15	0·17
Number of Teachers	41	−0·02	−0·04	−0·02	0·08	0·06	0·02
Attendance at School	42	0·19	0·12	0·19	0·08	0·01	0·21
Integration Rating	43	0·34	0·35	0·22	0·04	0·14	0·32
Attitude to Work Rating	44	0·37	0·28	0·39	0·27	0·19	0·48
General Ability Rating	45	0·52	0·34	0·41	0·30	0·18	0·55
Language Ability Rating	46	0·50	0·35	0·31	0·30	0·36	0·59
English Ability Rating	47	0·49	0·29	0·32	0·12	0·19	0·44
Arithmetic Ability Rating	48	0·52	0·31	0·43	0·33	0·13	0·52
Attitude to School	49	0·18	0·13	0·15	0·13	0·12	0·22
Attitude to Teacher	50	−0·08	0·05	−0·07	−0·03	0·07	−0·04
Social Adjustment	51	0·03	0·02	−0·02	0·04	0·00	0·03
Anxiety	52	0·09	0·17	−0·07	0·05	0·00	0·07
Importance of School Work	53	0·15	0·16	0·28	0·09	0·03	0·19

TABLE A2.1—*Continued*

	7	8	9	10	11	12	13	14	15	16
7	1·00									
8	0·25	1·00								
9	0·20	0·89	1·00							
10	0·21	0·71	0·67	1·00						
11	0·24	0·66	0·62	0·81	1·00					
12	0·42	0·14	0·11	0·17	0·12	1·00				
13	0·45	0·16	0·15	0·15	0·13	0·76	1·00			
14	0·56	0·31	0·26	0·32	0·31	0·51	0·42	1·00		
15	0·23	0·11	0·11	0·13	0·17	0·14	0·24	0·22	1·00	
16	0·17	-0·16	-0·14	-0·03	-0·05	0·14	0·07	0·15	0·13	1·00
17	-0·16	-0·01	-0·01	-0·10	0·01	-0·09	-0·03	-0·19	-0·16	0·10
18	0·02	-0·05	-0·10	-0·08	-0·08	-0·04	0·01	-0·15	0·19	-0·01
19	0·35	0·68	0·61	0·61	0·60	0·28	0·27	0·41	0·17	-0·14
20	0·35	0·67	0·60	0·62	0·62	0·29	0·26	0·41	0·16	-0·03
21	0·42	0·65	0·59	0·62	0·58	0·36	0·38	0·47	0·16	-0·02
22	0·54	0·41	0·33	0·46	0·44	0·37	0·40	0·57	0·28	0·02
23	0·40	0·55	0·50	0·44	0·39	0·35	0·39	0·44	0·23	0·03
24	0·44	0·49	0·46	0·46	0·41	0·32	0·33	0·46	0·29	-0·02
25	0·36	0·37	0·35	0·38	0·33	0·24	0·34	0·34	0·18	-0·05
26	0·08	0·01	0·00	-0·02	-0·12	0·03	-0·05	0·03	-0·05	-0·19
27	0·05	-0·03	0·01	0·05	-0·04	-0·11	-0·07	-0·13	-0·05	0·06
28	-0·03	0·12	0·15	0·09	0·05	-0·10	-0·05	-0·05	0·15	-0·05
29	0·06	0·09	0·06	-0·08	-0·06	0·00	-0·01	-0·14	-0·05	-0·06
30	-0·05	0·09	0·11	0·12	0·13	0·01	0·02	-0·10	0·09	0·01
31	-0·05	0·14	0·10	-0·04	0·05	-0·01	0·13	-0·05	0·04	-0·16
32	0·07	0·27	0·23	0·25	0·22	0·06	0·09	0·13	0·12	0·00
33	-0·19	0·01	-0·01	0·05	0·07	0·02	0·02	-0·13	-0·03	0·08
34	0·00	0·23	0·15	0·03	0·08	0·04	0·10	0·02	0·05	-0·24
35	0·20	0·18	0·05	0·13	0·18	-0·04	0·07	0·07	0·05	-0·01
36	0·36	0·34	0·35	0·30	0·33	0·30	0·30	0·34	0·34	0·09
37	0·18	0·29	0·24	0·26	0·31	0·17	0·13	0·30	0·04	-0·12
38	0·21	0·09	0·04	0·14	0·07	0·08	0·13	0·16	0·04	-0·05
39	0·05	0·06	0·11	0·00	0·02	0·03	0·08	0·09	0·18	-0·02
40	-0·08	0·10	0·09	0·05	0·08	0·02	-0·02	-0·03	0·00	0·09
41	-0·01	-0·20	-0·19	-0·19	-0·19	0·19	0·07	0·16	-0·01	0·09
42	0·18	0·12	0·11	0·13	0·20	0·20	0·22	0·31	0·05	-0·21
43	0·30	0·31	0·29	0·30	0·40	0·29	0·30	0·35	0·26	0·09
44	0·43	0·30	0·25	0·31	0·35	0·29	0·28	0·55	0·34	0·05
45	0·50	0·52	0·43	0·50	0·51	0·30	0·36	0·53	0·31	-0·03
46	0·42	0·45	0·38	0·45	0·46	0·32	0·31	0·49	0·23	-0·08
47	0·40	0·49	0·44	0·46	0·44	0·25	0·32	0·39	0·38	-0·09
48	0·53	0·44	0·36	0·40	0·40	0·37	0·43	0·64	0·36	0·01
49	0·27	0·21	0·21	0·21	0·16	0·22	0·18	0·27	0·24	-0·06
50	-0·08	0·07	0·00	0·12	0·10	-0·02	-0·04	-0·04	0·07	0·00
51	0·05	-0·03	-0·05	-0·04	-0·01	-0·02	-0·03	0·03	0·03	-0·05
52	0·09	0·09	0·06	0·17	0·14	0·04	0·03	0·09	0·07	-0·19
53	0·44	0·32	0·23	0·32	0·29	0·25	0·25	0·38	0·09	0·04

TABLE A2.1—*Continued*

	17	18	19	20	21	22	23	24	25	26
17	1·00									
18	−0·05	1·00								
19	−0·10	−0·06	1·00							
20	−0·03	0·03	0·92	1·00						
21	−0·10	0·01	0·88	0·93	1·00					
22	−0·32	−0·07	0·53	0·48	0·50	1·00				
23	−0·06	−0·16	0·63	0·66	0·69	0·49	1·00			
24	−0·16	−0·09	0·64	0·63	0·71	0·49	0·67	1·00		
25	−0·22	−0·22	0·41	0·40	0·42	0·48	0·39	0·37	1·00	
26	−0·20	0·05	−0·01	−0·05	−0·01	−0·04	0·08	0·15	−0·06	1·00
27	0·01	−0·02	−0·05	−0·04	0·02	0·01	0·06	0·12	0·07	0·15
28	−0·07	0·16	0·03	0·06	0·10	0·09	0·01	0·11	0·08	0·17
29	0·11	0·05	0·03	0·00	−0·01	−0·07	0·04	0·01	−0·08	−0·04
30	0·20	0·08	0·11	0·16	0·15	−0·08	0·09	0·15	−0·16	0·09
31	0·04	0·13	0·01	0·01	0·05	0·04	0·08	0·12	0·01	0·15
32	0·05	0·07	0·20	0·25	0·27	0·21	0·28	0·33	0·15	0·02
33	0·12	0·24	0·01	0·06	0·08	−0·13	0·11	0·11	−0·14	−0·02
34	−0·01	0·06	0·12	0·08	0·13	0·07	0·19	0·24	0·06	0·19
35	−0·06	0·11	0·19	0·18	0·18	0·30	0·16	0·25	0·26	−0·06
36	−0·03	0·01	0·33	0·31	0·33	0·41	0·39	0·38	0·34	−0·05
37	−0·13	0·00	0·36	0·34	0·39	0·33	0·29	0·37	0·22	0·10
38	−0·06	0·07	0·14	0·13	0·15	0·23	0·13	0·12	0·18	0·12
39	−0·07	−0·08	0·12	0·11	0·05	0·15	0·16	0·25	0·04	0·05
40	0·09	0·13	0·03	0·10	0·10	−0·17	0·23	0·24	0·03	0·09
41	−0·11	0·00	−0·17	−0·12	−0·09	0·04	−0·02	0·00	−0·09	0·10
42	−0·19	−0·34	0·27	0·21	0·22	0·21	0·24	0·16	0·19	0·11
43	−0·03	0·11	0·40	0·41	0·45	0·32	0·38	0·56	0·31	0·11
44	−0·11	0·03	0·43	0·40	0·43	0·53	0·37	0·36	0·56	−0·06
45	−0·21	0·01	0·59	0·58	0·60	0·66	0·55	0·56	0·71	−0·01
46	−0·06	0·07	0·60	0·58	0·65	0·42	0·58	0·59	0·56	0·08
47	−0·18	0·02	0·59	0·55	0·56	0·53	0·47	0·48	0·61	−0·02
48	−0·21	−0·09	0·49	0·44	0·52	0·68	0·49	0·50	0·61	0·01
49	−0·15	0·15	0·33	0·34	0·36	0·36	0·27	0·32	0·35	0·28	0·04
50	−0·02	0·21	0·08	0·13	0·06	0·08	−0·02	0·04	0·08	−0·05
51	0·00	−0·16	0·04	0·02	0·00	0·22	0·03	0·07	0·10	−0·05
52	0·00	−0·07	0·28	0·26	0·24	0·20	0·16	0·12	0·06	−0·05
53	−0·16	0·06	0·31	0·32	0·34	0·41	0·26	0·35	0·37	−0·05

TABLE A2.1—*Continued*

	27	28	29	30	31	32	33	34	35	36
27	1·00									
28	0·52	1·00								
29	0·03	0·00	1·00							
30	0·25	0·09	0·16	1·00						
31	0·17	0·24	0·16	0·12	1·00					
32	0·01	−0·01	0·17	0·11	0·47	1·00				
33	0·16	0·14	0·11	0·01	0·32	0·27	1·00			
34	0·07	0·07	0·17	0·06	0·71	0·68	0·39	1·00		
35	0·00	0·09	−0·08	−0·07	0·23	0·22	0·07	0·24	1·00	
36	0·01	0·00	−0·07	−0·09	−0·06	0·15	−0·11	0·01	0·21	1·00
37	0·00	0·15	−0·06	−0·14	0·03	0·14	0·01	0·07	0·31	0·48
38	0·15	0·17	−0·04	0·09	0·06	0·02	0·09	0·00	0·14	0·10
39	−0·17	−0·07	0·09	0·04	0·06	0·20	0·12	0·10	0·02	−0·04
40	0·14	0·10	0·17	0·20	0·12	0·23	0·27	0·21	−0·02	−0·05
41	−0·13	−0·08	−0·23	−0·07	−0·12	0·01	0·11	0·03	−0·08	−0·04
42	−0·12	−0·17	−0·07	−0·14	−0·06	0·03	−0·13	0·05	−0·06	0·10
43	0·05	0·15	0·15	0·07	0·18	0·28	0·18	0·26	0·11	0·20
44	−0·03	0·04	−0·09	−0·07	−0·12	0·08	−0·12	−0·04	0·10	0·39
45	0·01	0·12	−0·11	−0·05	−0·01	0·19	−0·04	0·09	0·28	0·47
46	0·09	0·10	−0·06	0·07	0·00	0·21	0·10	0·15	0·19	0·31
47	0·03	0·15	−0·06	−0·03	0·01	0·11	−0·06	0·05	0·22	0·43
48	0·00	0·12	−0·13	−0·13	−0·01	0·15	−0·13	0·05	0·19	0·49
49	0·06	0·05	0·10	0·22	0·02	0·13	−0·10	0·04	0·20	0·25
50	0·14	0·13	0·09	0·10	−0·11	−0·11	0·06	−0·08	0·11	0·00
51	0·03	0·11	−0·03	0·04	0·12	−0·06	−0·06	0·09	−0·01	0·04
52	0·06	0·13	−0·01	−0·09	0·09	0·09	0·04	0·11	0·19	0·18
53	−0·04	0·02	0·02	−0·10	−0·06	0·05	−0·02	−0·01	0·31	0·18

TABLE A2.1—*Continued*

	37	38	39	40	41	42	43	44	45	46
37	1·00									
38	0·16	1·00								
39	−0·03	−0·10	1·00							
40	−0·02	−0·12	0·02	1·00						
41	0·03	0·07	−0·01	0·00	1·00					
42	0·23	−0·01	0·15	−0·10	0·16	1·00				
43	0·23	0·13	0·16	0·17	0·09	0·13	1·00			
44	0·32	0·22	0·03	−0·07	0·01	0·29	0·36	1·00		
45	0·37	0·29	0·08	−0·03	−0·04	0·29	0·47	0·77	1·00	
46	0·37	0·21	0·04	0·26	−0·04	0·26	0·55	0·57	0·72	1·00
47	0·28	0·21	−0·01	−0·02	−0·14	0·26	0·45	0·67	0·81	0·71
48	0·34	0·23	0·01	−0·10	0·01	0·33	0·44	0·75	0·83	0·66
49	0·23	0·07	0·05	0·05	−0·05	0·21	0·16	0·34	0·35	0·29
50	0·09	−0·01	0·02	0·07	0·00	−0·03	0·09	0·13	0·14	0·08
51	−0·02	−0·07	0·17	−0·06	0·08	0·10	0·04	0·14	0·10	−0·03
52	0·08	0·10	0·03	−0·04	0·04	0·22	−0·06	0·12	0·20	0·12
53	0·25	0·12	0·02	−0·08	−0·03	0·04	0·38	0·42	0·46	0·32

TABLE A2.1—*Continued*

	47	48	49	50	51	52	53
47	1·00						
48	0·79	1·00					
49	0·26	0·27	1·00				
50	0·06	−0·01	0·23	1·00			
51	0·11	0·13	0·06	0·15	1·00		
52	0·13	0·15	0·28	0·03	0·12	1·00	
53	0·39	0·39	0·35	0·26	0·09	0·08	1·00

TABLE A2.2: *Correlation matrix of pupil variables 2: English sample*

		1	2	3	4	5	6
WISC Picture Completion	1	1·00					
WISC Picture Arrangement	2	0·47	1·00				
WISC Block Design	3	0·40	0·50	1·00			
WISC Object Assembly	4	0·35	0·39	0·61	1·00		
WISC Coding	5	−0·03	0·04	0·08	−0·10	1·00	
WISC Performance Scale I.Q.	6	0·65	0·68	0·81	0·67	0·33	1·00
WISC Vocabulary(Initial Testing)	7	0·30	0·38	0·38	0·11	0·05	0·36
Analogies	8	0·50	0·55	0·57	0·50	0·26	0·69
Verbal Learning Objects 1	9	0·13	0·24	0·22	0·21	0·02	0·19
Verbal Learning Objects 2	10	0·24	0·14	0·19	0·15	0·03	0·18
Verbal Learning Syllables 1	11	0·17	0·21	0·02	−0·06	0·14	0·14
Verbal Learning Syllables 2	12	0·05	0·08	0·00	−0·10	0·20	0·08
Concept Formation 1	13	0·01	0·07	0·17	−0·06	0·23	0·10
Concept Formation 2	14	0·17	0·04	0·24	0·14	0·32	0·27
Number Series	15	0·43	0·42	0·64	0·52	0·08	0·63
Draw-A-Man	16	0·27	0·31	0·44	0·47	0·02	0·45
Schonell Reading Age	17	0·37	0·38	0·17	0·06	0·10	0·33
Holborn Scale: Reading Age	18	0·43	0·37	0·23	0·07	0·13	0·36
Holborn Scale: Comprehension	19	0·43	0·37	0·25	0·08	0·16	0·37
Staffordshire Arithmetic	20	0·26	0·41	0·38	0·35	0·14	0·44
English Picture Vocabulary	21	0·49	0·41	0·44	0·25	−0·05	0·44
WISC Vocabulary	22	0·38	0·49	0·41	0·11	0·13	0·42

Table A2.2—*Continued*

	7	8	9	10	11	12	13	14	15	16
7	1·00									
8	0·53	1·00								
9	0·31	0·27	1·00							
10	0·33	0·26	0·85	1·00						
11	0·43	0·19	0·43	0·53	1·00					
12	0·38	0·19	0·29	0·41	0·84	1·00				
13	0·24	0·35	0·05	0·01	0·07	−0·05	1·00			
14	0·06	0·39	−0·04	−0·09	−0·03	−0·09	0·72	1·00		
15	0·34	0·75	0·35	0·27	0·20	0·23	0·36	0·56	1·00	
16	0·36	0·44	0·22	0·17	0·06	−0·06	0·18	0·22	0·37	1·00
17	0·45	0·41	0·53	0·52	0·66	0·61	0·20	0·19	0·51	0·06
18	0·45	0·47	0·61	0·63	0·61	0·51	0·30	0·21	0·52	0·14
19	0·51	0·49	0·59	0·62	0·63	0·53	0·31	0·25	0·54	0·13
20	0·31	0·62	0·42	0·40	0·23	0·19	0·41	0·32	0·66	0·40
21	0·39	0·35	0·31	0·33	0·27	0·28	0·08	0·17	0·40	0·19
22	0·70	0·55	0·39	0·43	0·37	0·32	0·33	0·14	0·42	0·35

Table A2.2—*Continued*

	17	18	19	20	21	22
17	1·00					
18	0·94	1·00				
19	0·92	0·97	1·00			
20	0·49	0·52	0·53	1·00		
21	0·44	0·50	0·53	0·31	1·00	
22	0·53	0·62	0·66	0·58	0·56	1·00

TABLE A2.3: *Inter-correlations of scoring methods of the learning tests*

Scoring Method	Indian Children N = 125				English Children N = 40			
Analogies:								
(1) Initial Score	1·00				1·00			
(2) Final Score	0·91	1·00			0·89	1·00		
(3) Gain Score	0·10	0·50	1·00		0·01	0·45	1·00	
Verbal Learning Objects:								
(1) Score on Learning Trials	1·00				1·00			
(2) Score on Retest	0·90	1·00			0·85	1·00		
(3) Score on Last Learning Trial	0·90	0·89	1·00		0·87	0·74	1·00	
(4) Score on First Retest Trial	0·86	0·95	0·83	1·00	0·81	0·93	0·67	1·00
Verbal Learning Syllables:								
(1) Score on Learning Trials	1·00				1·00			
(2) Score on Retest	0·81	1·00			0·84	1·00		
(3) Score on Last Learning Trial	0·86	0·77	1·00		0·88	0·81	1·00	
(4) Score on First Retest Trial	0·77	0·94	0·74	1·00	0·79	0·97	0·75	1·00
Concept Formation:								
(1) No. of Prompts Subtracted from 50	1·00				1·00			
(2) No. of Spontaneous Classifications	0·74	1·00			0·72	1·00		
(3) No. of Classifications on Set 6	0·34	0·42	1·00		0·24	0·20	1·00	
Concepts 2 + *Concepts 3*	0·70				0·66			
Concepts 2 + 4 × *Concepts 3*	0·54				0·43			
Number Series:								
(1) Completion of Series	1·00				1·00			
(2) Filling in Series	0·56				0·57			
Memory:								
(1) Total Number Remembered	1·00				1·00			
(2) Memory Span	0·56				0·54			

TABLE A2.4: *Eigen values and variance of eight learning test scores, intelligence tests and criterion scores*

EIGEN VALUES	VARIANCE %
8·60	43·0
2·58	55·9
1·60	63·9
1·13	69·5
0·98	
0·77	
0·67	
0·62	
0·56	
0·51	
0·37	
0·37	
0·32	
0·28	
0·20	
0·16	
0·10	
0·09	
0·05	
0·03	

TABLE A2.5: *Correlations between the oblique primary factors of the eight learning tests scores, intelligence tests and criterion scores*

Factor				
1	1·00			
2	0·53	1·00		
3	0·53	0·57	1·00	
4	0·11	0·18	0·10	1·00

TABLE A2.6: *Oblique primary factor loadings of eight learning test scores*

VARIABLE	1	2	3
1. Verbal Learning Objects 1	−0·93	0·06	−0·05
2. Verbal Learning Objects 2	−0·94	0·08	−0·14
3. Verbal Learning Syllables 1	−0·87	−0·04	0·06
4. Verbal Learning Syllables 2	−0·83	−0·12	0·15
5. Analogies	0·07	0·02	0·90
6. Concept Formation 1	0·00	0·91	0·03
7. Concept Formation 2	−0·02	0·91	0·03
8. Number Series	−0·05	0·04	0·84

G

TABLE A2.7: *Summary table of regression analyses. Percentages of variance explained*

1. HOLBORN SCALE READING AGE STEP 1	1	2	3	4	5
Regression A					
All Variables					
Verbal Learning Objects 1	44	40	26	25	—
WISC Picture Arrangement	—	10	10	8	—
Verbal Learning Syllables 1	—	—	19	17	—
Number Series	—	—	—	6	—
Total	44	50	55	56	—
Regression B					
Learning Scores and Teacher's Estimate					
Verbal Learning Objects 1	44	30	28	—	—
Verbal Learning Syllables 1	—	19	17	—	—
Number Series	—	—	6	—	—
Total	44	49	51	—	—
Regression C					
Intelligence Scores and Teacher's Estimate					
WISC Performance Scale IQ	16	12	7	1	—
Teacher's Estimates	—	11	11	10	11
WISC Picture Arrangement	—	—	9	9	9
WISC Picture Completion	—	—	—	8	9
Total	16	23	27	28	29

2. HOLBORN SCALE: COMPREHENSION STEP 1	1	2	3	4	5
Regression A					
All Variables					
Verbal Learning Objects	43	37	25	25	23
Number Series	—	14	13	9	7
Verbal Learning Syllables 1	—	—	16	16	16
Concept Formation 2	—	—	—	7	7
WISC Picture Arrangement	—	—	—	—	6
Total	43	51	54	57	59
Regression C					
Intelligence Scores and Teacher's Estimate					
WISC Picture Completion	22	18	15	—	—
Teacher's Estimates	—	13	12	—	—
WISC Picture Arrangement	—	—	7	—	—
Total	22	31	34	—	—

TABLE A2.7—*Continued*

3. STAFFORDSHIRE ARITHMETIC	STEP 1	2	3	4	5
Regression A					
All Variables					
Number Series	33	26	23	16	16
Teacher's Estimates	—	16	12	9	9
Verbal Learning Syllables 1	—	—	11	11	11
Analogies	—	—	—	13	13
WISC Object Assembly	—	—	—	—	4
Total	33	42	46	49	53
Regression C					
Intelligence Scores and Teacher's Estimate					
Teacher's Estimates	23	19	18	—	—
WISC Picture Completion	—	11	9	—	—
WISC Object Assembly	—	—	8	—	—
Total	23	30	35	—	—

4. ENGLISH PICTURE VOCABULARY	STEP 1	2	3	4	5	6
Regression A						
All Variables						
Verbal Learning Objects 1	30	23	22	22	22	21
WISC Performance Scale IQ	—	21	17	12	8	3
Concept Formation 2	—	—	8	8	9	8
WISC Picture Arrangement	—	—	—	8	6	8
WISC Object Assembly	—	—	—	—	6	8
WISC Picture Completion	—	—	—	—	—	9
Total	30	44	47	50	51	57
Regression B						
Learning Scores and Teacher's Estimate						
Verbal Learning Objects 1	30	27	24	—	—	—
Concept Formation 2	—	12	9	—	—	—
Number Series	—	—	9	—	—	—
Total	30	39	42	—	—	—
Regression C						
Intelligence Scores and Teacher's Estimate						
WISC Performance Scale IQ	28	18	11	8	—	—
WISC Picture Completion	—	15	15	14	—	—
WISC Picture Arrangement	—	—	11	10	—	—
Teacher's Estimates	—	—	—	8	—	—
Total	28	33	37	40	—	—

TABLE A2.8: *Regression analysis using verbal learning objects and number series only*

PERCENTAGE OF VARIANCE EXPLAINED

Criterion	Verbal Learning Objects	Number Series	VLO & NOS Combined	
Holborn Scale Reading Age	44	17	VLO	40
			NOS	9
			Total	49
Holborn Scale Comprehension	43	22	VLO	37
			NOS	14
			Total	51
Staffordshire Arithmetic	17	33	VLO	11
			NOS	28
			Total	39
English Picture Vocabulary	30	19	VLO	25
			NOS	13
			Total	38

TABLE A2.9: *Children with zero scores on the Holborn reading and comprehension scale: correlations of final scores with the learning test scores*

TEST	ACCURACY N = 16		COMPREHENSION N = 31	
	Correlation Coefficient	Level of Significance	Correlation Coefficient	Level of Significance
1. Verbal Learning Objects 1	0·15	NS	0·30	NS
2. Verbal Learning Objects 2	0·28	NS	0·33	NS
3. Verbal Learning Syllables 1	0·41	NS	0·47	1%
4. Verbal Learning Syllables 2	0·43	5%	0·52	1%
5. Analogies	0·17	NS	0·31	NS
6. Concept Formation 1	0·33	NS	0·33	NS
7. Concept Formation 2	0·39	NS	0·27	NS
8. Number Series	0·22	NS	0·30	NS

TABLE A2.10: *Kolmogorov-Smirnov tests for English—Indian differences on the learning ability, intelligence and criterion scores*

TEST	D	χ_2^2	LEVEL OF SIGNIFICANCE
Learning Ability:			
Analogies	0·50	29·94	0·1%
Verbal Learning Objects 1	0·38	17·32	0·1%
Verbal Learning Objects 2	0·36	15·62	0·1%
Verbal Learning Syllables 1	0·18	3·80	NS
Verbal Learning Syllables 2	0·20	4·80	NS
Concept Formation 1	0·25	7·82	5%
Concept Formation 2	0·30	10·98	1%
Number Series	0·35	15·19	0·1%
Intelligence:			
WISC Picture Completion	0·31	11·65	1%
WISC Picture Arrangement	0·53	34·57	0·1%
WISC Block Design	0·38	17·69	0·1%
WISC Object Assembly	0·41	20·08	0·1%
WISC Coding	0·08	0·74	NS
WISC Performance Scale I.Q.	0·41	19·98	0·1%
Draw-a-Man	0·12	1·86	NS
Criterion:			
Schonell Reading	0·35	14·43	0·1%
Holborn Scale Reading Accuracy	0·38	17·23	0·1%
Holborn Scale Comprehension	0·43	22·32	0·1%
Staffordshire Arithmetic	0·26	8·12	5%
WISC Vocabulary	0·57	39·22	0·1%

TABLE A2.11: *Kolmogorov-Smirnov tests for sex differences in the attainments of Indian children*

TEST	INITIAL ATTAINMENTS χ_2^2	FINAL ATTAINMENTS χ_2^2
Schonell Reading Test	2·10	0·66
Holborn Reading Scale	0·65	0·68
Holborn Comprehension	0·45	0·77
Staffordshire Arithmetic	1·45	2·34
English Picture Vocabulary	2·34	3·64
WISC Vocabulary	3·07	2·93

(None of these values reaches the level of significance at a 5% level)

TABLE A2.12: *Means t- and F-values for 10 school, class and teacher variables on criterion tests*

1. *School Group:* Group 1 = 18% Indians and 32% Immigrants or less
   Group 2 = more than 18% Indians and 32% Immigrants

CRITERION TEST	MEANS		t-Value
	Group 1	Group 2	
1. Schonell Reading	34·68	34·85	−0·07
2. Holborn Reading Accuracy	10·09	10·15	−0·06
3. Holborn Comprehension	7·89	8·26	−0·51
4. Staffordshire Arithmetic	13·02	13·38	−0·25
5. English Picture Vocabulary	16·77	19·25	−1·87
6. WISC Vocabulary	22·02	23·53	−1·15

(None of these values reaches significance)

2. *Teacher's Attitudes : Factor Scale A:* Group 1 = Score 52 or less
   Group 2 = Score 53–58
   Group 3 = Score 59 or more

CRITERION TEST	MEANS			F-Value
	Group 1	Group 2	Group 3	
1. Schonell Reading	32·69	38·29	35·54	1·63
2. Holborn Reading Accuracy	9·11	11·45	10·57	2·23
3. Holborn Comprehension	7·22	9·29	8·14	2·74
4. Staffordshire Arithmetic	11·92	14·74	12·80	1·30
5. English Picture Vocabulary	16·64	19·58	17·63	1·62
6. WISC Vocabulary	21·19	24·50	22·54	2·08

(None of these values reaches significance)

TABLE A2.12—*Continued*

3. *Teacher's Attitudes: Factor Scale B:*   Group 1 = Score 53 or less
   Group 2 = Score 54–59
   Group 3 = Score 60 or more

| CRITERION TEST | MEANS | | | |
	Group 1	*Group 2*	*Group 3*	*F-Value*
1. Schonell Reading	35·59	34·85	36·16	0·08
2. Holborn Reading Accuracy	10·49	9·82	10·81	0·37
3. Holborn Comprehension	8·23	7·97	8·49	0·15
4. Staffordshire Arithmetic	12·59	12·09	14·78	1·24
5. English Picture Vocabulary	16·18	18·03	19·84	2·52
6. WISC Vocabulary	22·62	22·09	23·57	0·39

(None of these values reaches significance)

4. *Teacher's Attitudes: Factor Scale C:*   Group 1 = Score 40 or less
   Group 2 = Score 41 or more

| CRITERION TEST | MEANS | | |
	Group 1	*Group 2*	*t-Value*
1. Schonell Reading	34·63	36·30	−0·64
2. Holborn Reading Accuracy	10·04	10·67	−0·67
3. Holborn Comprehension	8·13	8·33	−0·27
4. Staffordshire Arithmetic	13·63	12·84	0·53
5. English Picture Vocabulary	17·08	18·69	−0·15
6. WISC Vocabulary	22·23	23·21	−0·72

(None of these values reaches significance)

TABLE A2.12—*Continued*

5. *Teacher's Attitudes: Total Score:* Group 1 = Score 152 or less
Group 2 = Score 153 or more

| CRITERION TEST | MEANS | | *t-Value* |
	Group 1	Group 2	
1. Schonell Reading	33·27	38·37	−1·97
2. Holborn Reading Accuracy	9·58	11·39	−1·93
3. Holborn Comprehension	7·65	8·96	−1·75
4. Staffordshire Arithmetic	12·40	14·14	−1·16
5. English Picture Vocabulary	16·37	19·96	−2·58*
6. WISC Vocabulary	21·60	24·22	−1·92

(* = Significant at the 5% level)

6. *Frequency of Testing Reading Over Two Years:* Group 1 = 5 times or less
Group 2 = More than 5 times

| CRITERION TEST | MEANS | | *t-Value* |
	Group 1	Group 2	
1. Schonell Reading	34·35	35·47	−0·43
2. Holborn Reading Accuracy	9·84	10·60	−0·82
3. Holborn Comprehension	7·69	8·70	−1·34
4. Staffordshire Arithmetic	13·89	11·93	1·32
5. English Picture Vocabulary	17·49	18·56	−0·78
6. WISC Vocabulary	22·19	23·58	−1·03

(None of these values reaches significance)

TABLE A2.12—*Continued*

7. *Frequency of Testing Reading in Year Two:* Group 1 = twice or less
   Group 2 = 3 times or more

	CRITERION TEST	MEANS		
		Group 1	*Group 2*	*t-Value*
1.	Schonell Reading	35·67	34·13	0·61
2.	Holborn Reading Accuracy	10·29	10·00	0·32
3.	Holborn Comprehension	8·50	7·76	1·01
4.	Staffordshire Arithmetic	14·44	12·31	1·46
5.	English Picture Vocabulary	19·83	16·54	2·45*
6.	WISC Vocabulary	23·35	22·24	0·83

(* = Significant at the 5% level)

8. *Frequency of Testing Arithmetic Over Two Years:* Group 1 = 3 or more times in each year
   Group 2 = 3 or more times in year 2 only
   Group 3 = twice or less in year 2

	CRITERION TEST	MEANS			
		Group 1	*Group 2*	*Group 3*	*F-Value*
1.	Schonell Reading	32·05	34·94	37·05	1·42
2.	Holborn Reading Accuracy	9·03	9·67	11·49	2·92
3.	Holborn Comprehension	7·33	7·64	9·07	2·38
4.	Staffordshire Arithmetic	13·79	11·28	14·21	1·61
5.	English Picture Vocabulary	17·10	16·64	19·63	2·11
6.	WISC Vocabulary	21·26	21·81	24·74	2·99

(None of these values reaches significance)

TABLE A2.12—*Continued*

9. *Frequency of Testing Spelling Over Two Years:* Group 1=3 or more times in
each year

Group 2=3 or more times in
year 2 only

Group 3=twice or less in year 2

| CRITERION TEST | MEANS | | | |
	Group 1	Group 2	Group 2	F-Value
1. Schonell Reading	30·89	36·71	36·03	2·20
2. Holborn Reading Accuracy	8·44	10·63	11·23	3·32*
3. Holborn Comprehension	6·92	8·47	8·71	2·30
4. Staffordshire Arithmetic	12·58	13·16	13·90	0·24
5. English Picture Vocabulary	16·36	18·22	19·10	1·34
6. WISC Vocabulary	20·86	23·00	24·32	2·11

(* = Significant at the 5% level)

10. *Years of Teaching Experience:* Group 1=5 years or less for teachers in each
year

Group 2=6 years or more in year 1; 5 years or
less in year 2

Group 3=6 years or more in year 2

| CRITERION TEST | MEANS | | | |
	Group 1	Group 2	Group 3	F-Value
1. Schonell Reading	36·26	37·14	32·00	1·41
2. Holborn Reading Accuracy	10·81	10·43	9·66	0·52
3. Holborn Comprehension	8·53	8·35	7·69	0·46
4. Staffordshire Arithmetic	11·79	14·51	14·19	1·46
5. English Picture Vocabulary	18·05	18·68	17·25	0·34
6. WISC Vocabulary	22·95	23·51	22·22	0·28

(None of these values reaches significance)

TABLE A2.13: *Correlation matrix of nine learning test scores on the initial Indian sample*

		1	2	3	4	5	6	7	8	9
Verbal Learning Objects 1	1	1·00								
Verbal Learning Objects 2	2	0·89	1·00							
Verbal Learning Syllables 1	3	0·71	0·67	1·00						
Verbal Learning Syllables 2	4	0·67	0·64	0·81	1·00					
Concept Formation 1	5	0·19	0·15	0·16	0·14	1·00				
Concept Formation 2	6	0·19	0·17	0·17	0·15	0·73	1·00			
Analogies	7	0·28	0·23	0·24	0·28	0·43	0·47	1·00		
Number Series	8	0·33	0·28	0·35	0·34	0·47	0·44	0·57	1·00	
Memory	9	0·31	0·25	0·33	0·33	0·15	0·22	0·34	0·33	1·0

APPENDIX THREE

Notes on the Principal Components Analysis

by Jill M. Tarryer

THE purpose of the principal components analyses which were undertaken in this research was to reduce the original variables to a smaller number of interpretable factors. The number of components which were extracted for rotation to simple structure was determined by the number of Eigen values which were greater than one. Two rotations were applied. First a Varimax rotation was used to obtain orthogonal simple structure from which an oblique solution was obtained by the Promax procedure (Hendrickson *et al.*, 1966). The oblique solution was preferred to the orthogonal alternative because the correlated factors model was considered to be more appropriate to the data.

Principal components analysis was applied to four correlation matrices. An account of the statistical techniques may be found in *Modern Factor Analysis* (Harman, 1960); the computer programme used to obtain the results was the factor analysis programme from the IBM 1130 Statistical System.

Two of the matrices were based on the results of the 118 Indian children who completed the research. These are in fact sub-matrices of the large correlation matrix which is given in Table A2.1. Both analyses followed straightforward courses, and since the results have been given in some detail in the text there is no need for further discussion here.

The other two analyses were carried out at an early stage in the research. These were based on the results of the 125 Indian children who were tested with the learning tests. A correlation matrix was formed from the scores on nine of the tests—the eight which were listed on page 46 plus score 1 on the Memory test which was later discarded. Two factors were extracted from this matrix. The Memory test score had an extremely low communality of 0·27 and also low loadings of both factors. These factors revealed that there was an underlying difference between the Verbal Learning tests and the remaining tests.

As a result of these findings the Memory test was deleted from the matrix and a further principal components analysis was undertaken with the stipulation that three factors were to be extracted regardless of the size of the Eigen values. The largest three Eigen values were found to be 3·85, 1·95 and 0·71 so that the three largest components accounted for 84 per cent of the variance of these eight scores. The expected split between the verbal and non-verbal scores was evident from the results which also revealed a secondary division within the non-verbal tests. The Number Series test was more closely related to the analogies score than to the concept scores which were themselves closely related (Table A2.6). The secondary importance of this division is also demonstrated by the correlations between the oblique primary factors (−0·18 between factors 1 and 2; −0·30 between factors 1 and 3 and 0·51 between factors 2 and 3). The correlation matrix for the 125 children is given in Table A2.13. There were no substantial differences from the correlations which are reported in Table A2.1.

APPENDIX FOUR

Description of the Tests of Verbal Learning Ability

Verbal Learning 1. Learning the names of objects

The child is given eight timed trials in which to learn the names of six objects. A record is kept of the number of successful responses he has been able to make during the course of these learning trials and he is given two trials the following day to see how well he has remembered these names over a longer period of time.

Administration of the Test

Thirty-one objects are spread out at random on the table, in front of the child, and their names are said by the examiner in the following order:

funnel	spill	beaker	tube	strainer
candle	whisk	screw	string	doily
wire	flex	hinge	taper	plug
reel	dice	nib	peg	chisel
ribbon	file	spanner	dart	domino
dummy	pliers	jigger	spool	bobbin
bodkin				

The purpose of this part of the test is to ascertain which of the object names the child can recognize. The child is encouraged to touch the objects he knows when the examiner says the names, by the examiner giving an inquiring look and by touching the first object himself if the child fails to respond.

All the objects except six whose names were unknown are removed. These six are chosen on the basis of three having two-syllable names, three having only one-syllable names and no two names should sound too much alike, e.g. spool and spill. These precautions are taken so as to equate the task as far as possible for each child.

The examiner arranges the six objects in a row in front of the child, so that the one- and two-syllable names alternate. He then points to each object in turn from left to right, saying their names and encouraging the child to repeat each one in turn after him. It is necessary to say an object's name again if the child's pronunciation is very indistinct and this process should be repeated until the child's pronunciation of the word is recognizable. This part of the procedure is untimed.

Eight trials are given for learning the names. The examiner points to each object in turn at an approximate rate of one every three seconds. If the child cannot recall the name, the examiner prompts him, the child saying the name again after him. Only the original optimum pronunciation is accepted, e.g. not baker or flox when the child has been able to say beaker and flex.

On the fifth trial, the order of the objects is changed at random and kept in this new order for the rest of the learning trials. This is to ensure that the child is learning by the paired associate method and not in a meaningless rote-like fashion.

The test may be discontinued after the fifth trial if the child has achieved three successive error-free trials. He is then credited with the remaining number of responses.

The child is re-tested the following day, when two trials are given and the objects are presented according to the same procedure in their original order.

Scoring

1. Number of correct responses during the eight trials of the learning period.

2. Number of correct responses on both trials of the period of recall.

Verbal Learning 2. Learning of nonsense syllables

This task involves the learning of nonsense syllables by the method of serial anticipation. As with the previous tests there are eight timed trials with two further trials the following day.

The list of eight syllables is as follows:[1]

NID	BOF
ZOM	YIL
PUV	FEP
KEX	WUG

[1] The nonsense syllables were selected from the list of syllables with low association values prepared by Melton from the studies of Glaze, Hull and Krueger (see Stevens, S.S., 1958, p. 539). They were selected on the basis of being pronounceable, of three letters only and with no obvious association in Punjabi.

Another list of eight syllables was prepared to be used in the re-tests for reliability and if necessary could be used as a parallel item. This second list is as follows:

RUX	TEV
GAW	JUF
YOL	ZAN
MIB	BIP

Each syllable is written in block capitals on separate plain white non-transparent cards measuring $5\frac{1}{2}$ in. $\times$ $3\frac{1}{2}$ in.

Administration of the Test

The syllables are presented to the child by the method of serial anticipation, at the rate of one every three seconds. There is an eight-second gap between each trial and eight learning trials are given altogether. The initial run-through is not timed and is not counted in the eight learning trials. The examiner says the name of the syllable while the child looks at the same syllable written on the card. Sometimes it is necessary, as in the learning of the names of the objects, to get the child to repeat a syllable and for the examiner to repeat the syllable in order to obtain a recognizable pronounciation from the child. This initial run-through is not presented according to regular timing.

Having presented the whole list once, the examiner then indicates by a questioning look and pointing to the top card, which is face downwards on the pile, that the child must guess the first syllable. If he has not guessed after three seconds, the examiner turns the card face upwards and says it to him, indicating that the child is to repeat it, and so on through the list.

As in the first verbal learning test, the test continues up to the 8th trial unless the child manages three successive trials without error in which case the test is discontinued and he is credited with the remaining items. The child is re-tested the following day when two trials are given.

Scoring

1. Number of correct responses during the eight trials of the learning period.

2. Number of correct responses on both trials of the period of recall.

Analogies

This test consists of 13 different analogies, each represented by a pair of geometric figures drawn on a separate sheet of paper. The analogies are based on the following underlying relationships; they increase in difficulty and are presented in the following order:

1. Unshaded—shaded
2. Small—large
3. One—two
4. Empty—duplicate figure inside
5. Mirror image joined on at side
6. Addition of another line
7. Corners made round
8. Inside out
9. In front—behind and vice versa
10. Filling in gap and change of position through 90°
11. Figures made squat and to overlap
12. Larger figure turned upside down and duplicate put inside at base.
13. Subtraction of side and closing up of figure.

Underneath each pair of figures there is room for two further pairs, but the second figure of each of these is missing and the child has to draw the missing figures in accordance with the principle of association which exists between the top pair of figures. Further completed examples of each analogy are available for teaching purposes.

Administration of the Test

The examiner places the first sheet of drawings in front of the child and indicates by pointing first to the left and then the right hand drawing in the top pair of drawings, and then to the drawings below and the spaces beside them, that the child is to draw in the missing figures with the pencil he now hands to him.

This test is not timed, so the child is allowed as much time as he needs to make the drawings. If he fails to grasp what is required of him, or he gives up or makes incorrect drawings, the examiner shows him the three teaching examples which belong to the first analogy, pointing from the left to the right hand figure in each pair until the child appears to understand. The 'teaching sheet' is removed out of sight and the child is then given a further chance on a new sheet of paper to complete the original items. If the child still fails, the examiner draws in the correct figures, before proceeding to the second analogy.

The remaining analogies are administered in the same way, each with their own teaching examples when required. All 13 analogies are given unless the child fails four consecutive analogies, in which case the test is discontinued.

In all cases, the child must be allowed to finish both drawings or do as much as he can. The examiner should then indicate by nodding or shaking his head to each of the child's drawings which of them are right or wrong before proceeding either with the teaching examples or with the next analogy, but no indication should be given about success or failure until the child has finished both drawings.

Scoring

The score is equal to the total number of points obtained with the aid of the teaching examples during the course of the test. Specific criteria were evolved for the scoring of each analogy, but in general, one point is given for successful completion of both drawings of an analogy, and half points were given for partially correct responses on the more difficult items.

Concept formation

In this test there are six sets of wooden and plastic shapes of various design, size and colour which are to be sorted from an oblong tray into round transparent containers spread out in the front of the child (four of the latter are required during the course of the test). Round objects, beads, were chosen for the first set of material to be sorted so that the child would not be distracted away from the purpose of the test into using the material for building towers, steps or making patterns, thereby establishing the appropriate kind of 'set' for the test. Uneven numbers of objects are presented for classification so that the child can in no way continue to hold the impression that the objects are to be divided into equal groups.

Administration of the Test

Set One

Materials: 5 white and 7 blue beads. These beads are to be sorted into 2 containers.

The examiner places the oblong tray in front of the child and puts the beads into it. Two containers are placed at the side of the tray nearer to the child and the examiner indicates by general gestures of the hand from the beads to the containers that the beads are to be removed from the trays into the containers. As much help, correction and repetition as is necessary is given by the examiner at this stage, if necessary by placing some of the beads himself, until he is sure the child has grasped the idea of sorting the beads according to their colour. This is the only way in which this first set of material can be sorted.

The number of prompts required at this stage is not included in the test scores. The purpose of this first stage is to familiarize the child with the idea that he is to sort objects from the tray into containers. Some children may have had a great deal of experience with this activity in the classroom and it would be penalizing unfairly those children who had had no such experience to include the number of prompts necessary at this stage in the final score. The experience of the children may thus be considered to have been more nearly equated when they are presented with the second set of materials.

Set Two

Materials: 9 large round beads: 3 white, 4 green, 2 black
10 small round beads: 3 white, 3 green, 4 black

These beads are to be sorted:

a)   into three containers according to colour and

b)   into two containers according to size.

The beads are placed in the tray and the examiner indicates that they are to be sorted into three containers. The only way this can be achieved is by sorting according to colour. If the child seems uncertain as to what is expected of him, the examiner should place one bead, and if necessary another bead, all the time encouraging the child to do so himself.

Each time a bead is placed or corrected by the examiner, one point is added to the score of prompts. When the first sorting has been completed, the beads are returned to the tray and one of the containers is removed, the examiner indicating by gestures that the beads are now to be sorted into only two containers. The only way this can be done is to sort them according to their size. Again, prompts are given when necessary. A record is also kept of any classifications spontaneously achieved without the examiner's help.

This set of material has introduced the idea that the same objects can be sorted in more than one way.

111

Set Three

Materials: Large and small flat plastic discs in 4 colours:

2 large yellow;	3 small yellow
2 large green;	2 small green
1 large blue;	3 small blue
1 large red;	1 small red

These discs are to be sorted into:

    a)   2 containers according to size, and

    b)   4 containers according to colour.

The purpose of this item is to consolidate the connection between number of containers and number of categories required in the classification. First two and then four containers are placed in front of the child.

The procedure is the same as for the second set of material. A record is kept of the number of prompts and spontaneously achieved classifications.

Set Four

Materials: 13 flat plastic shapes of 3 designs and in 3 colours:

2 yellow diamonds;	1 yellow square;	2 yellow circles
1 green diamond;	1 green square;	2 green circles
1 red diamond;	2 red squares;	1 red circle

This material is to be sorted:

    a)   according to shape, and

    b)   according to colour.

Three containers are required for each sorting and the sortings may be made in either order, so that when it is necessary for the child to be urged to continue or correct a piece the examiner should place the piece in accordance with the hypothesis which the child appears to have in mind. If the examiner has to begin the first classification for the child, it does not matter which of the two criteria the examiner selects.

The aim of this item is to convey the idea of sorting the same material in two ways, although the same number of containers are provided each time, i.e. the child has the opportunity to learn that the first method of sorting which he has selected is not to be repeated.

A record is kept of the number of prompts required and spontaneous classifications achieved.

Set Five

Materials: White and grey wooden blocks of 2 sizes and thicknesses:

3 large thick white blocks, one with grey sides
3 large thin white blocks, one with grey sides
3 small thick white blocks, two with grey sides
4 small thin white blocks, two with grey sides

These blocks are to be sorted into two containers according to:

a) size
b) thickness and
c) colour of sides

The sortings may be made in any order and the procedure is the same as for the fourth set of material. This task gives further practice in changing the principle of sorting even though the number of containers remains the same. By using white blocks of two different sizes and thicknesses, some of which have grey sides, practice is given in classifying the blocks according to two criteria, thickness and sides, not used with the previous items.

Again a record is kept of the number of prompts required and spontaneous classifications achieved.

Set Six

Materials: 10 wooden pieces of different shape, size, colour, thickness and side-colouring:

1 large thick blue square with black sides
1 large thick green square with same coloured sides
1 large thin blue square with same coloured sides
1 small thick white square with black sides
1 small thick green triangle with black sides
1 large thin white triangle with black sides
1 large thick white trapezium with black sides
1 large thin blue trapezium with same coloured sides
1 large thin green trapezium with same coloured sides
1 small thin green trapezium with black sides

This material is to be sorted:

a) into three containers twice, according to shape and colour and

b) into two containers three times; according to sides, size and thickness.

The general procedure is the same as for the fourth and fifth sets of material, except that no help is given in attaining the classifications *unless* an otherwise correct sorting has been spoiled by one piece incorrectly placed. In this case, the examiner should point to the incorrectly placed piece, shaking his head to indicate that it is wrong. If the child spontaneously and immediately corrects the error, the classification is then scored as being correct.

Every child is given the same number of opportunities of sorting into three containers and two containers, even if he is sorting the pieces in a random or otherwise incorrect fashion.

No prompts are given in this part of the test, so that the only score for this item is the number of spontaneous classifications achieved.

The five preceding tasks have provided each child with an equal opportunity for knowing what is required of him on this last set of material. An equal amount of practice has been afforded to each child in sorting the previous material according to the criteria provided with the sixth set of material; this last task is, therefore, a situation in which the child's ability to benefit from previous learning situations may be assessed.

Scoring

Score 1=Total number of prompts on 2nd, 3rd, 4th and 5th sets of material. *This total must then be subtracted from 50.* Higher scores are thus indicative of a superior response to this test than lower scores.

Score 2=Number of correct sortings achieved without help on the 2nd–5th sets of material.

Score 3=Number of correct sortings achieved on the 6th set of material.

Number series

Shaw's (1962) 'Structa' Arithmetic Apparatus appeared to be the most suitable material for this test. It was chosen for its attractiveness and because graduated series could be arranged without any difficulty by children of this age.

The test is arranged in two parts: (a) Completion of Series, and (b) Filling-in Series, and the entire test is given to all children. Materials required are one 'Structa' peg board and 50 'Structa' pegs of one colour.

Administration of the Test

(a) *Completion of series.* The examiner demonstrates how the pegs fit into each other and into the peg board, and places a graduated series of 1, 2 and 3 pegs along a single row of holes in the peg board. The examiner indicates that the child must complete the next two in the series, i.e. put some pegs into the next two holes. If the child fails to grasp the idea or puts in the wrong number of pegs, the examiner must indicate this by shaking his head. The examiner puts them right and, for this first item, indicates to the child by pointing that he must complete the next two in the same series. When the child has completed 2 items, the examiner removes all the pegs and constructs the first 2 items in the next series. For each of the following five series, the examiner indicates by pointing to the peg box and to the appropriate holes that the child is to complete the next 2 items in each of the series. Where he fails the examiner himself puts in the appropriate number of pegs before proceeding to the next item.

The child is required to complete the next 2 items in the following series:

Number of Pegs

1.	1	3	–	–
2.	6	5	–	–
3.	3	6	–	–
4.	8	6	–	–
5.	10	7	–	–

(b) *Filling-in series.* Again the examiner places two of the items, but in this part of the test these are not in successive order. The child has to place the missing two items in the following series:

Number of Pegs

1.	1	–	5	–
2.	2	–	–	8
3.	–	4	–	10
4.	12	–	–	3

The examiner indicates into which holes the child should place the pegs. It does not matter in which order the child fills the holes in any of the series. When he has finished placing pegs in both holes, if both are incorrect the examiner should correct the first of the child's items, and should point to the second of the child's items with an enquiring look at the child to see if he spontaneously corrects this without further help. In the case where only one of the child's items was wrong, the examiner should indicate that it was wrong and again give the child a chance to correct it before doing so himself and passing on to the next series.

Scoring

The score is equal to the number of correct responses on the two parts of the test combined: for every item of the Completion of Series including the first demonstration item, one point is given for each correct response (the range of scores on this part of the test is 0–12); for the Filling-in Series, both items in a series must be correct to score one point (the range of scores in this part of the test is 0–4).

Bibliography

ALLEYNE, H. M. (1962). 'The effect of bilingualism on performance in certain intelligence and attainment tests'. Unpublished MA thesis, University of London.

ANASTASI, A. and FOLEY, J. P. (1949). *Differential Psychology*. New York: Macmillan.

ANNETT, M. (1959). 'The classification of instances of four common class concepts by children and adults', *Brit. J. Educ. Psychol.*, **29**, 3, 223-36.

BARKER LUNN, J. C. (1969). 'The development of scales to measure junior school childrens' attitudes', *Brit. J. Educ. Psychol.*, **39**, 1, 64-71.

BARKER LUNN, J. C. (1970). '*Streaming in the Primary School*'. Slough: NFER.

BERNSTEIN, B. (1961). 'Social structure, language and learning', *Educ. Res.*, **3**, 3, 163-76.

BIESHEUVEL, S. (1949). 'Psychological tests and their application to non-European peoples'. *Yearbook of Education*, 87-126. London: Evans Bros.

BIESHEUVEL, S. ed. (1969). *Methods for the Measurement of Psychological Performance*. IBP Handbook No. 10. Oxford and Edinburgh: Blackwell Scientific Publications.

BLOOM, B. S., DAVIS, A. and HESS, R. (1965). *Compensatory Education for Cultural Deprivation*. New York: Holt, Rinehart & Winston.

BRENT TEACHERS' ASSOCIATION AND WILLESDEN AND BRENT FRIENDSHIP COUNCIL (1969). *Children in a Changing Community*. A report by the joint sub-committee of the Brent Teachers' Association and the Willesden and Brent Friendship Council.

BRIMER, M. A. and DUNN, L. M. (1963). *The English Picture Vocabulary Test*. Slough: NFER.

BUTCHER, H. J. (1968). *Human Intelligence, Its Nature and Assessment*. London: Methuen.

CRONBACH, L. J. (1951). 'Co-efficient Alpha and the internal structure of tests', *Psychometrika*, **16**, 297-334.

DEPARTMENT OF EDUCATION AND SCIENCE (1967). *Statistics of Education Volume 1 1966*. London: HM Stationery Office.

DEPARTMENT OF EDUCATION AND SCIENCE (1968). *Statistics of Education Volume 1 1967*. London: HM Stationery Office.

DEPARTMENT OF EDUCATION AND SCIENCE (1969). *Statistics of Education Volume 1 1968*. London: HM Stationery Office.

DEPARTMENT OF EDUCATION AND SCIENCE (1970). *Statistics of Education Volume 1 1969*. London: HM Stationery Office.

DERRICK, J. (1966). *Teaching English to Immigrants*. London: Longmans.

DEUTSCH, M. (1962). 'The disadvantaged child and the learning process'. In: PASSOW, A. H. *Education in Depressed Areas*. New York: Teachers College, pp. 163-79.

DRAPER, N. R. and SMITH, H. (1966). *Applied Regression Analysis*. New York: Wiley.

FERRON, O. (1965). 'The test performance of coloured children', *Educ. Res.*, **8**, 1, 42-57.

GARRETT, H. E. (1958). *Statistics in Psychology and Education*. 5th Ed. London: Longmans.

GOLDMAN, R. J. and TAYLOR, F. M., (1966). 'Coloured immigrant children: a survey of research studies and literature on their educational problems and potential—in Britain', *Educ. Res.*, **8**, 3, 163-84.

GOODENOUGH, F. L. and HARRIS, D. B. (1963). *Goodenough-Harris Drawing Test*. New York: Harcourt, Brace & World.

GUILFORD, J. P. (1957). *The Nature of Human Intelligence*. New York: McGraw-Hill.

HARMAN, H. H. (1960). *Modern Factor Analysis*. Chicago: University of Chicago Press.

HARRIS, D. B. (1963). *Childrens' Drawings as Measures of Intellectual Maturity*. New York: Harcourt, Brace & World.

HAYNES, J. M. (1970). 'The abilities of immigrant children. A study of the educational progress of 7-9-year-old Indian children.' Unpublished PhD thesis, University of London.

HEARNSHAW, L. S. (1951). 'Exploring the intellect', *Brit. J. Psychol.*, **42**, 4, 315-21.

HEBRON, M. E. (1958). *The Staffordshire Arithmetic Test*. London: Harrap.

HENDRICKSON, A. E. and WHITE, P. O. (1966). 'A method for the rotation of higher-order factors', *Brit. J. Statist. Psychol.*, **19**, 1, 97-103.

HESS, R. D. and SHIPMAN (1965). 'Early blocks to children's learning', *Children*, **12**, 189-94.

HOUGHTON, V. P. (1966). 'A report on the scores of West Indian immigrant children and English children on an individually administered test', *Race*, **8**, 1.

HOUSE OF COMMONS SELECT COMMITTEE ON RACE RELATIONS AND IMMIGRATION (1969). *The Problems of Coloured School Leavers*. London: HM Stationery Office.

INNER LONDON EDUCATION AUTHORITY (1967). *The Education of Immigrant Pupils in Primary Schools*. London: ILEA Report 959.

JENSEN, A. R. (1961). 'Learning abilities in Mexican, American and Anglo-American children', *California J. Educ. Res.*, **12**, 147-59.

JENSEN, A. R. (1963). 'Learning ability in retarded, average and gifted children, *Merrill-Palmer Quart.*, **9**, 123-40.

JENSEN, A. R. (1967a). 'The culturally disadvantaged: psychological and educational aspects'. *Educ. Res.*, **10**, 1, 4-20.

JENSEN, A. R. (1967b). 'Social class and verbal learning'. In: DEUTSCH, I.M., JENSEN A. R., and KATZ, I. eds. *Social Class, Race and Psychological Development*. New York: Holt, Rinehart & Winston.

JENSEN, A. R. (1968). 'Social class, race and genetics', *Amer. Educ. Res. J.*, **5**, 1, 1-42.

JENSEN, A. R. (1969). 'How much can we boost IQ and scholastic achievement?', *Harvard Educ. Rev.*, **39**, 1, 1-123.

JENSEN, A. R. and ROHWER, W. D. (1963). 'Verbal mediation in paired associate and serial learning', *J. Verbal Learning & Verbal Behav.*, 346-52.

JENSEN, A. R. and ROHWER, W. D. (1965). 'Syntactical mediation of serial and associate learning as a function of age', *Child Develop.*, **36**, 601-4.

KLINEBERG, O. (1935). *Negro Intelligence and Selective Migration*. New York: Columbia University Press.

118

Bibliography

LESSER, G. S., FIFER, G. and CLARK, D. H. (1965). 'Mental abilities of children from different social class and cultural groups', *Soc. Res. Child Develop.* **30**, 4.

LLOYD, F. and PIDGEON, D. A. (1961). 'The effects of coaching on non-verbal test material with European, Indian and African children', *Brit. J. Educ. Psychol.*, **31**, 2, 145-51.

LOVELL, K. (1955). 'A study of intellectual deterioration in adolescents and young adults', *Brit. J. Psychol.*, **46**, 3, 199-210.

MACKAY, G. W. S. (1962). 'A study of the prediction of learning ability in the primary school'. Unpublished MA thesis, University of London.

MACKAY, G. W. S. and VERNON., P. E. (1963). 'The measurement of learning ability', *Brit. J. Educ. Psychol.*, **33**, 2, 177-86.

MCARTHUR, R. S., IRVINE, S. H. and BRIMBLE, A. R. (1964). *The Northern Rhodesia Mental Ability Survey, 1963.* Lusaka: Rhodes-Livingstone Institute.

MCFIE, J. (1961). 'The effect of education on African performance on a group of intelligence tests', *Brit. J. Educ. Psychol.*, **31**, 3, 232-40.

MOELY, B., OLSON, F., HALWES, T. and FLAVELL, J. (1969). 'Production deficiency in young childrens' clustered recall', *Develop. Psychol.*, **1**, 1, 26-34.

MURPHY, L. J. (1957). 'Tests of abilities and attainments'. In: EWING, A. W. G., *Educational Guidance and the Deaf Child*, pp. 252-77. Manchester: Manchester University Press.

ORD, I. G. (1967). 'The New Guinea performance scale and its educational uses', *Papua & New Guinea J. Educ.*, **5**, 7-16.

ORTAR, G. R. (1960). 'Improving test validity by coaching', *Educ. Res.*, **2**, 3, 137-42.

OTTO, W. (1961). 'The acquisition and retention of paired associates by good, average and poor readers', *J. Educ. Psychol*, **52**, 241-248.

PAYNE, J. F. (1967). 'A comparative study of the mental ability of seven- and eight-year-old British and West Indian children in a West Midland town'. Unpublished thesis: University of Keele.

PIDGEON, D. A. (1970). *Expectation and Pupil Performance.* Slough: NFER, Slough.

PORTEUS, S. D. (1931). *The Psychology of a Primitive People.* New York: Longmans.

POWER, J. (1967). *Immigrants in School.* A survey of administrative policies. London: Councils and Education Press.

RIVERS, W. H. R. (1901). 'Vision'. In: HADDON, A. C. *Report of the Cambridge Anthropological Expedition to the Torres Straits*, Cambridge: Cambridge University Press.

ROBINSON, W. S. (1960). 'Ecological correlations and the behaviour of individuals', *Amer. Soc. Rev.*, **15**, 351-7.

ROSENTHAL, R. and JACOBSON, L. (1966). 'Teachers' expectancies, determinants of pupils' IQ gains', *Psychol. Reports*, **19**, 115-8.

SAINT, C. K. (1963). 'Scholastic and sociological adjustment problems of the Punjabi speaking children in Smethwick'. Unpublished MEd dissertation, University of Birmingham.

SCHOOLS COUNCIL (1967). *English for the Children of Immigrants.* Working Paper Number 13. London: HM Stationery Office.

SCHONELL, J. F. (1951). *Psychology and Teaching of Reading.* 3rd Ed. London: Oliver & Boyd.

119

SIEGEL, S. (1956). *Nonparametric Statistics: for the Behavioural Sciences.* McGraw-Hill. The Pennsylvania State University.

SCOTT, G. C. (1950). 'Measuring Sudanese intelligence', *Brit. J. Educ. Psychol.*, **20**, 1, 43-54.

SHAW, H. (1962). ' "Structa" Arithmetic Apparatus', *Mathematics Teaching*, **20**.

SOCIETY FOR THE PSYCHOLOGICAL STUDY OF SOCIAL ISSUES (1969). 'SPSSI Council statement on race and intelligence', *J. Soc. Issues.*, **25**, 3, 1-3.

STEVENS, S. S. (1958). *Handbook of Experimental Psychology.* New York: Wiley.

* THORNDIKE, R. L. (1968). Review of Rosenthall, R. and Jacobson, L. *Pygmalion in the Classroom.*, in *Amer. Educ. Res. J.*, **5**, 4, 708-11.

VERNON, P. E. (1940). *The Measurement of Abilities.* London: University of London Press.

VERNON, P. E. ed. (1957). *Secondary School Selection.* London: Methuen.

VERNON, P. E. (1969). *Intelligence and Cultural Environment.* London: Methuen.

WATTS, A. F. (1948). *The Holborn Reading Scale.* London: Harrap.

WECHSLER, D. (1949). *The Wechsler Intelligence Scale for Children.* New York: The Psychological Corporation.

WILSON, J. (1961). 'Film literacy in Africa', *Canadian Communications*, **1**, 7-14.

WOODROW, H. (1946). 'The ability to learn', *Psychol. Rev.*, **53**, 147-58.

Index